DEFOE DE-ATTRIBUTIONS

DEFOE DE-ATTRIBUTIONS

A CRITIQUE OF
J.R. MOORE'S *CHECKLIST*

P.N. FURBANK AND W.R. OWENS

THE HAMBLEDON PRESS
LONDON   AND   RIO GRANDE

Published by The Hambledon Press 1994
102 Gloucester Avenue, London NW1 8HX (U.K.)

P.O. Box 102, Rio Grande, Ohio 45674 (U.S.A.)

ISBN 1 85285 128 7

A description of this book is available from the British Library and from the
Library of Congress

Typeset, printed on acid-free paper and bound in Great Britain by Cambridge
University Press

Contents

For
Alan Downie

Preface

The standard authority on the canon of Defoe's works is John Robert Moore's *Checklist of the Writings of Daniel Defoe* (1960; second edition, Hamden, Connecticut, 1971), which lists some 570 separate titles. We believe that this vast assemblage of attributions to Defoe is altogether unrealistic, and the present book is an attempt to reassess it systematically. It lists and discusses 252 items in Moore which, in our view, ought not rightly to figure as part of Defoe's *oeuvre*. In many cases, we argue, no sound case has ever been made for the attribution, while in others there is positive evidence pointing towards another author. Our views on the formation of the Defoe canon, and our working methods and reasoning, are explained more fully in the Introduction which follows.

It should be noted that our book is primarily a discussion of each work from the point of view of its attribution and it does not offer full bibliographical descriptions. Titles are arranged according to the numbering sequence in Moore, but only short titles and brief details of publication are provided. All Moore numbers are printed in bold, including cross references to works not listed in the present book. Quotations usually follow the original exactly, but elsewhere punctuation and capitalisation within eighteenth-century titles have been regularised. In references to secondary works the place of publication is London except where otherwise indicated.

The work on which our book is based has stretched over a number of years, during which we have been assisted in different ways by various institutions and individuals.

We are grateful for financial assistance from the University and the Arts Faculty Research Committees of the Open University. W.R. Owens is grateful for travel and research grants from the British Academy.

We would also like to thank the following people for their help and encouragement: David Blewett; Val Buckland; Tony Coulson; Alan Downie; Simon Eliot; David Goldthorpe; David Hayton; Alan Johnson; Lawrence Kennedy; John McVeagh; Richard Ovenden; Mrs Yerevan Peterson; Rochelle Scholar; Ian Willison.

Abbreviations

Major Defoe Bibliographers

Chalmers
: George Chalmers's "List of Writings" of Defoe, appended to the second edition of his *Life of Daniel De Foe* (1790). It is in two parts: (1) "considered as undoubtedly De Foe's"; (2) "supposed to be De Foe's"

Crossley
: James Crossley's manuscript list of attributions drawn up between 1869 and 1883, reprinted in P.N. Furbank and W.R. Owens, *The Canonisation of Daniel Defoe* (New Haven and London, 1988), pp. 184–87

Hutchins
: Henry C. Hutchins's list of Defoe's writings in *The Cambridge Bibliography of English Literature* (1940)

Lee
: William Lee, *Daniel Defoe: His Life, and Recently Discovered Writings*, 3 vols. (1869), and the "Chronological Catalogue of Daniel Defoe's Works" at the beginning of vol. 1

Moore
: John Robert Moore, *A Checklist of the Writings of Daniel Defoe*, 2nd. edn. (Hamden, Connecticut, 1971). When not otherwise indicated, quotations from Moore are from his comments on a given item in his *Checklist*. We identify items by means of his running number. Moore marked certain of these numbers with an asterisk, to indicate that the attribution was uncertain; these asterisks are reproduced here

Novak   Maximillian E. Novak's list of Defoe's writings
                                  in *The New Cambridge Bibliography of English
                                  Literature* (1971)
Trent (Bibliography)   William Peterfield Trent's unpublished Biblio-
                                  graphy of Defoe, typescript now in the Col-
                                  lection of American Literature, Beinecke Rare
                                  Book and Manuscript Library, Yale University,
                                  New Haven, Connecticut
Trent (*CHEL*)   Trent's list of works at the end of his chapter on
                                  Defoe in the *Cambridge History of English Litera-
                                  ture*, ed. A.W. Ward and A.R. Waller, 14 vols.
                                  (1912), ix
Trent (*Nation*)   Trent's "Bibliographical Notes on Defoe, I-
                                  III" in the New York *Nation*, June-August 1907
Wilson   Walter Wilson's *Memoirs of the Life and Times of
                                  Daniel De Foe*, 3 vols. (1830), and the "Cata-
                                  logue of De Foe's Works" at the beginning of
                                  vol. 1

Other Abbreviations

BL   British Library
Canonisation   P.N. Furbank and W.R. Owens, *The Canonisation of Daniel
                  Defoe* (New Haven and London, 1988)
DNB   *Dictionary of National Biography*
HLQ   *Huntington Library Quarterly*
Letters   *The Letters of Daniel Defoe*, ed. George Harris Healey
                  (Oxford, 1955)
NCBEL   *The New Cambridge Bibliography of English Literature* (1971)
N & Q   *Notes and Queries*
PBSA   *Papers of the Bibliographical Society of America*
PQ   *Philological Quarterly*
Review   *Defoe's Review Reproduced from the Original Editions*, ed.
                  Arthur W. Secord, 22 vols. (New York, 1938)
RES   *Review of English Studies*

Introduction

In 1988 we published *The Canonisation of Daniel Defoe*. It is worth quoting the first few sentences from it here, since they still represent our views:

> The present book takes its rise from a feeling, which seems to be shared in varying degrees by a number of scholars, that the Defoe "canon" is a remarkably strange and not very satisfactory construction. It contains, indeed, as odd and as great an assortment of texts as, perhaps, has ever been attributed to one author, and for the larger part these texts have been ascribed on internal evidence alone. Can they really all be by Defoe?[1]

As we mentioned in our book: between 1790, when the first bibliography of Defoe appeared, and 1971, when John Robert Moore published the second edition of his *Checklist of the Writings of Daniel Defoe*,[2] the canon had swollen from just over a hundred items to 570. A large proportion of these attributions had been made in the nineteenth and twentieth centuries, on the basis of features of style, "favourite phrases", resemblance to Defoe's known views and the like; and it seemed to us, as it still does, that there may be something fundamentally unsound in this practice of ascribing works to an author, two or three centuries after his death, on the basis merely of internal evidence.

Over the last few decades various scholars, including Pat Rogers, Frank Ellis, Alan Downie, Spiro Peterson and Henry Snyder, have attacked particular attributions, often conclusively;[3] and in 1974, in the course of a savage critique of J.R. Moore's arguments for Defoe's authorship of *Robert*

---

[1] P.N. Furbank and W.R. Owens, *The Canonisation of Daniel Defoe* (New Haven and London, 1988), p.1.

[2] J.R. Moore, *A Checklist of the Writings of Daniel Defoe* (Bloomington, Indiana, 1960; second edition, Hamden, Connecticut, 1971).

[3] For details, see section VI "Discussions of the Canon" in John A. Stoler, *Daniel Defoe: An Annotated Bibliography of Modern Criticism, 1900–1980* (New York and London, 1984).

Drury's Journal, Rodney Baine called for a root-and-branch re-examination of the canon.[4]

We vaguely considered undertaking such a re-examination ourselves, but the prospect seemed too daunting, and for the time being we gave up thoughts of a full-scale investigation. Then in 1991 we accepted an invitation to compile the "Defoe" entry in the forthcoming new edition of the *Cambridge Bibliography of English Literature* (*CBEL3*); and, having done so, it seemed to us logical that we should eventually use this as a basis for a new full-scale checklist, in which we could trace the history and rationale for each attribution.

What then became obvious to us was that, if we were to follow the principles of attribution spelled out in *The Canonisation of Daniel Defoe*, we should be having to drop a considerable (perhaps an alarming) number of items from the current canon, including probably some very familiar ones – on the grounds, not so much that they could not be by Defoe, as that no good case had ever been put forward for their being so. But this presented us with a problem. If we made these omissions *silently*, without explanation, would we not be exposing ourselves to the same criticism as we had often levelled at others? It was one of our chief complaints in the book that whatever Defoe bibliographers had done in the past, in the way of assigning new works to Defoe, had for the most part been done silently. Here, we argued, had been a great source of misunderstanding, and indirectly a cause of the prodigious swelling of the canon. For the bare presence of an item in a bibliographer's list, without explanation, tends to give it an aura of authority, as if there must be some very good reason for its being there, and all the more so if it is carried over into some later list. (The principle of inertia is as important in bibliography as it is in Newtonian physics.) Further, when a given work has, by sheer persistence, won a secure foothold in the canon, it is natural for bibliographers to regard it as a warrant for attributing other works of the same genre. "Silent" attribution has been the bane of Defoe bibliography, but silent de-attribution would be almost as bad.

Something could be done in answer to this problem, of course, in the form of articles questioning particular attributions or groups of attributions, but this would hardly be enough. A more systematic solution seemed to be called for, and that is the origin of the present work. It is a list of all the items in Moore's *Checklist* (the current authority on the Defoe canon) that at present we consider questionable, with, in the case of each

---

[4] Rodney M. Baine, "Daniel Defoe and Robert Drury's *Journal*", *Texas Studies in Literature and Language*, 16 (1974), 479–91.

work, a note as to who (so far as we can discover) was the first to attribute it to Defoe, a very brief synopsis, and an explanation of our reasons for doubting the ascription. As will be found, these reasons are very various. In certain cases we can refer the reader to some already published discussion of the attribution, by others or by ourselves. In others we bring forward new evidence which casts doubt on the ascription. In others again we register sheer incomprehension as to why the work ever got assigned to Defoe. And in certain further cases we admit the plausibility of Defoe's having written the work – its general compatibility with his prose-style and outlook and so on – but argue that something more is needed, some scrap of external evidence or compelling piece of internal evidence, to warrant a "probable" attribution. (We have not attempted to deal with periodicals, since they would call for more detail than there is room for. It is one of the many weaknesses of Moore's *Checklist* that it makes a blanket ascription of certain journals to Defoe, when at most he contributed only certain items, or perhaps was merely the editor or proprietor.)

Thus *Defoe De-Attributions* is designed as an adjunct to, and partial justification for, our forthcoming list in *CBEL3* and our projected new checklist of Defoe's writings. It comes out a year or two in advance of these, and this will give other scholars the chance to offer corrections and disagreements or to let us know of evidence we were not aware of. If we have erred on the side of severity in our judgements, this will at least have one advantage. It will mean that, when we classify an item as "probably by Defoe", we can do so with a comfortable sense that we mean the phrase literally, and not merely as a loose synonym for "possibly by Defoe" or "sometimes attributed to Defoe".

The History of Defoe Attribution

How the Defoe canon arrived at its present shape and enormous dimensions is a long and curious tale, depending in considerable measure on the character and preoccupations of the six bibliographers who made the largest contribution to it: George Chalmers (1742–1825), Walter Wilson (1781–1847), William Lee (1812–*c*.1890), James Crossley (1800–1883), William Peterfield Trent (1862–1939) and John Robert Moore (1890–1973). We sketched the activities of these six in a certain amount of detail in *The Canonisation of Daniel Defoe*, and in the next part of the present Introduction we do our best to fill in the rest of the story, beginning with the various attributions to Defoe made during his own lifetime. In this historical section our main focus will be on the all-important question of

the *transmission* of attributions. Following this, in the third part of the
Introduction, we discuss the principles and methods of author-attribution.

Attributions Made during Defoe's Lifetime

Defoe for much of his career published anonymously and many anonymous
works were attributed to him during his lifetime. It was a favourite theme
of his enemies that he was a mercenary hack, capable of writing on both
sides of an issue; and he was frequently provoked into complaining both at
specific attributions to him and at the general tendency to father all
ownerless pamphlets on him. "Whenever any Piece comes out which is not
liked", he writes in his apologia *An Appeal to Honour and Justice* (1715), "I
am immediately charg'd with being the Author, and very often the first
Knowledge I have had of a Books being publish'd, has been from seeing
my self abused for being the Author of it, in some other Pamphlet publish'd
in Answer to it."[5] In our notes on particular items in the present work, we
have recorded such contemporary ascriptions as we are aware of.

Two important contemporary attributors of works to Defoe may
perhaps be given particular mention here. In the *Political State* for June
1717, the month in which Defoe's erstwhile employer the Earl of Oxford
was tried and acquitted for treason, Defoe's rival and enemy Abel Boyer
delivered a violent attack on Defoe, describing him as "a Scribler famous
for Writing upon, for, and against all manner of Persons, Subjects and
Parties".

> This Man has formerly put his NAME to some of his *Low-Productions*, but having been
> stigmatized by an *ignominious Punishment*, he has since conceal'd it with all possible
> Industry, and, at the same Time, prostituted his Pen to the *vilest Purposes*. He was
> thought a fit Tool for the Designs in Hand, by those who had the Administration of
> Affairs during the Four last Years of the last Reign; who, among other *dirty Work*, put
> him upon Writing a Weekly-Paper call'd MERCATOR, calculated to procure an easy
> Passage to a Bill, by which a great Branch of the Trade of *Great-Britain* was to have been
> given up. The Beneficence of his Masters, and in particular of the E-- of O--, enabled
> him to repair and beautify his Habitation at *Newington*, where he had set up his FORGE
> of *Politicks* and *Scandal*, from which, for these Six Years past, he supplies *Monthly*, often
> *Weekly*, the *Publishers* in and about *Paternoster-Row*.

Boyer then proceeded to ascribe fourteen anonymous works to Defoe. The
list, as given in the *Political State*, is as follows (with Moore numbers
inserted in square brackets):

1. *The Secret History of the* WHITE-STAFF, in 3 Parts [**280, 282, 298**]. 2. *A Secret History of
One Year* [**283**]. 3. *Advice to the People of* Great-Britain, *with respect to Two important*

[5] Defoe, *An Appeal to Honour and Justice* (1715), p. 25.

Questions, 1. *What they ought to expect from the King?* 2. *How they ought to behave to him?* [**281**]. 4. *An Account of the Conduct of* Robert *Earl of* Oxford [**323**]. 5. *Impeachment or no Impeachment* [**285**]. 6. *The Folly and Vanity of Impeaching.* 7. *An Account of the Two Nights Court at* Greenwich [**334**]. 8. *An Account of a Conference at* S--t *House* [**354**]. 9. *A Letter to the Right Hon.* Robert Walpole, *Esq* [?**370**]. 10. *Some National Grievances represented.* 11. *An* Argument *against Employing and Ennobling Foreigners*, in 2 Parts [**359, 369**]. 12. *An Account of the Conduct of the Lord Viscount* Townshend [**358**]. 13. *Mercurius Politicus*, (or *Monthly Scandal* upon the Present Government.) [**533**]. 14. And lastly, *Minutes of the* Negotiations *of Monsieur* Mesnager [**377**].[6]

Twelve of these attributions, it will be seen, have survived into Moore's *Checklist*, and we deal with six of them below.

Less well known than Boyer, but perhaps in the long run no less influential as a Defoe attributor, was Robert Wodrow (1679–1734), a Scottish Presbyterian divine, best remembered for his two-volume *History of the Sufferings of the Church of Scotland from the Restoration to the Revolution* (1721–22). Wodrow was an avid collector of books and manuscripts, and, since many of the contemporary pamphlets he bought were of course anonymous, it was his habit to inscribe what he took to be the author's name on the title-page. He subsequently had many of these pamphlets bound up in volumes, with his own handwritten list of contents, including details of authorship, at the front.

In 1791, Wodrow's enormous library was sold by his son to the Advocates' Library of Edinburgh (a large part of which was subsequently transferred to the National Library of Scotland). Early in the nineteenth century, a manuscript "Catalogue of the Wodrow Pamphlets" was prepared, presumably by one of the librarians.[7] The compiler arranged works under author and subject headings, evidently drawing upon Wodrow's title-page ascriptions. The "Defoe" entry is worth reproducing faithfully and in full, with Moore numbers following in square brackets. (It will be seen that the list includes a few items attacking or otherwise referring to Defoe; we have placed these in square brackets.)

On occasional Conformity of Dissenters. Lond. 1701. 4 [i.e. quarto]. V. Howe [**17**]
Letter to Mr. Howe. Ib. 1701. 4 [**31**]
The trueborn Englishman. Ib. 1701. 4 [**28**]
Test of the Church of England's Loyalty. 1702. 4 [**44**]
On prejudices against a Union. pp. [i.e. parts] 3, 4, 5, 6. 1706. 4 [**120, 124, 138, 139**]
On the Excise after the Union. 1706 [***130**]
[Remarks on the above. 4]

[6] *The Political State*, June 1717, pp. 632–33.
[7] See folio volume, FR. 207, in the National Library of Scotland.

The State of the Excise vindicated. 4 [*131]
On the fifth article of Union. 4 [125]
[The advantages of the Act of Security. 1706. 4]
The advantages of Scotland by an Union. 1706. 4 [134]
[The Preface to the above considered. V. Black (W)]
On the Equivalent. 1706. 4 [136]
[An Equivalent for Defoe – a Poem. 4]
Answer to Lord Haversham's Speech. 15 Feb. 1707. Fol. [145]
Presbyterian persecution examined. Edin. 1707. 4 [152]
A sixth Essay. 1707. 4 [139]
Voice from the South. 1707. 4 [148]
View of the Protestant Religion in Britain. Edin. 1707. 4 [146]
The Scots Narrative examined. Lond. 1709. 4. V. Greenshields. [160]
[A Reprimand to. [sic] Edin. 1710. 4]
Vindication of – Ib. 1710. 4 [?166]
On Sacheverel's Sermon. Lond. 1710. 12 [i.e. duodecimo] [?171]
Insinuations of, in favour of the Pretender. Ib. 1712. 8 [i.e. octavo] [172]
Union or no Union. Ib. 1713. 12 [255]
[The true-born Englishwoman. 1703. 8]
[Reflections on the shortest way with dissenters. 1703. 4]
The Mock-mourners. Lond. 1702. 8 [42]
Now or never. 4⁸
An Advertisement to Mr. Clark. 4 [167]
Answer to Dyer's Letter. 4 [153]
Letter to the Glasgowmen. 4 [132]
The Rabbler convicted. 4 [133]
Letter from Reason to the Mob. 4 [121]
The dissenters vindicated. 4 [140]

Of this list, eight items may be described as first-time attributions by Wodrow, in the sense that, by writing "By Dan. De Foe" or some such phrase on his copies, he was the earliest person to associate them with Defoe (a fact of particular significance in that several of these attributions were put into general circulation in the printed catalogue of the Advocates' Library published in 1873). The eight items we refer to are Moore numbers **121, 125, *130, *131, 133, 134, 136, 145**. It is rather striking that in the case of the first seven, the *only* evidence of Defoe's authorship offered by Moore is the existence of an "old manuscript note" on the title-page of the copy in the National Library of Scotland. Plainly he had not realised that these notes are all in the same hand, and that the hand is Wodrow's. In our view, only numbers **125** and **136** can safely be accepted, and we explain our reasons for rejecting the other six below. As regards Wodrow's general reliability in these matters, it is significant that another work attributed by him to Defoe, but not in the list above, was the famous *Advice to the Electors of Great Britain* (1708), and Moore once again cites the "old manuscript note" in the National Library copy: "By D. De Foe. May. 11. 1708". It has, however, been established beyond doubt that this tract is not by Defoe – there being in existence a manuscript of the work in the hand of Arthur Maynwaring – so it is clear that Wodrow's ascriptions should be treated with some scepticism. (See our note on **156** below.)

Mid Eighteenth-Century Attributions

The first significant list of Defoe's works compiled after his death appeared in 1753 in Cibber's *Lives of the Poets* – a work in fact, according to the testimony of Samuel Johnson, written by the Scotsman Robert Shiels.[9] Shiels mentions twenty-two works, saying that

> His principal performances, perhaps, are these,
>
> *A Plan of Commerce*, an esteemed Work ...
> *Memoirs of the Plague*, published in 1665
> *Religious Courtship*
> *Family Instructor*. Two Volumes
> *History of Apparitions* (under the name of Moreton)
> *Robinson Crusoe*. Two Volumes
> *Political History of the Devil*
> *History of Magic*
> *Caledonia*, a Poem in praise of Scotland
> *De Jure Divino*, a Poem
> *English Tradesman*, etc.
> *History of Colonel Jack*
> *Cleveland's Memoirs*, etc. are also said to be his.'[10]

The next important step in Defoe attribution occurred when, in the 1770s, Francis Noble, proprietor of a fashionable circulating library in Holborn and a leading publisher of fiction, had the inspiration of exploiting Defoe as a circulating-library novelist.[11] He had already published some

---

[8] This is presumably *Now or Never: or, A Looking-Glass for the Representatives of the People ... Written by an Asserter of Liberty and Property* (London, 1702).

[9] See Johnson's "Life" of James Hammond: "Of Mr. Hammond ... I was at first able to obtain no other memorials than such as are supplied by a book called *Cibber's Lives of the Poets*; of which I take this opportunity to testify that it was not written, nor, I believe, ever seen by either of the Cibbers; but was the work of Robert Shiels, a native of Scotland, a man of very acute understanding, though with little scholastic education, who, not long after the publication of his work, died in London of a consumption ... Theophilus Cibber, then a prisoner for debt, imparted, as I was told, his name for ten guineas. The manuscript of Shiels is now in my possession."

[10] T. Cibber, *Lives of the Poets of Great Britain and Ireland, to the Time of Dean Swift*, 5 vols. (1753), iv, 313–25.

[11] For an account of Noble's activities as publisher of Defoe see our "Defoe and Francis Noble", *Eighteenth-Century Fiction*, 4 (1992), 301–13.

Defoe works (or what we have come to think of as such) without ascribing them to an author: a *Moll Flanders* in 1741; a *History of the Great Plague* in 1754 (in the advertisement pages of which there is listed a *Roxana*); and a *Captain Singleton* in 1768. But now it evidently dawned on him that Defoe's name might be a draw, and that the ancient and disreputable *Moll Flanders*, *Roxana* and the like might be rewritten and rendered suitable for a genteel readership. Accordingly, in 1775 he issued a metamorphosed *History of Mademoiselle de Beleau; or, The New Roxana*, described on its title-page as "Published by Mr. Daniel Defoe. And from papers found, since his decease, it appears was greatly altered by himself"; and in the following year he published an equally transmogrified *Moll Flanders*. This, so far as we know, was the first time that Defoe's name had appeared on the title-page of a novel, an event of considerable significance. The venture was evidently a commercial success and seems to have led Noble to ask himself whether Defoe had not written more novels, or perhaps had written works hitherto taken as authentic histories but which were in fact works of fiction, or could be passed off as such. The end-result may be seen in Noble's catalogue of 1787, where various Defoe titles have been neatly homogenised:

> De Foe's Adventures of a Cavalier
> De Foe's Adventures of Roxana
> De Foe's Adventures of Moll Flanders
> De Foe's Adventures of Captain Singleton
> De Foe's History of the Great Plague in London
> De Foe's Voyage Round the World by a Course Never sailed before.

It was this Noble episode which really launched the modern idea of Defoe as a novelist. When the Scottish antiquary George Chalmers published a *Life of Daniel De Foe* in 1785 he was taken to task by a correspondent named "Borealis" in the *Gentleman's Magazine* (November, 1789) for not knowing that Defoe was the author of the *New Voyage Round the World*, the *History of Roxana*, *Memoirs of a Cavalier* and the *History of Moll Flanders*, works so much "in vogue amongst country readers". It would be safe to assume that "Borealis" was taking his cue from Francis Noble's title-pages and library-catalogues; and when in 1790 Chalmers came to publish a "List of Writings, which are considered as undoubtedly De Foe's", he took the admonition and included those items.

The full importance of Noble's activities for the history of Defoe attribution can be judged from his edition of *Daniel Defoe's Voyage Round the World by a Course Never Sailed Before* (1787). It included a "Life of the Author" by an imaginary "William Shiells", plagiarised from the "Life" of 1753 by Robert Shiels. The list of publications in the latter – which contained only one work of fiction apart from *Robinson Crusoe*, i.e. *The History of Colonel Jack* – has been doctored to reflect Noble's recent publishing exploits and now reads as follows:

It is impossible to arrive at a knowledge of half the productions of this ingenious man, as he never put his name to any. However, it is now well known the following agreeable works are a part of his performance.

History of Robinson Crusoe
Voyage Round the World by a Course Never Sailed Before. Describing the manners
    of the Chilian Indians, a people till then entirely unknown to the Europeans
Life and Adventures of Captain Singleton
Life of Roxana; or, The Fortunate Mistress
Life of Laetitia Atkins; or, Moll Flanders
Life of Colonel Jack
History of the Great Plague in London
Religious Courtship
Family Instructor
History of Apparitions
Political History of the Devil
History of Magic

With many others, that are only to be met with in the libraries of the curious.

There follows a note by the "EDITOR':

The Reader is desired to observe, in this work, as in all his other writings, Mr. Daniel De Foe ever chose to conceal his name, and left it to the public to discover the author. For his genius was so extremely prolific, and his imagination so lively, that in every description of adventure, in any of his works of fancy, both by sea and land, he adhered so closely to nature, that no one had the least suspicion of their being merely inventions, but founded upon real truths; until Mr. Shiells, the writer of his life, which is here prefixed, and never before published in any his works, gave a catalogue of his writings, as far as he could collect them, and which is confirmed, concerning the present work, as a fiction by the ingenious Mr. Forster, in his Voyages and Discoveries in the North printed in 1786, where he says, speaking of a pretended discovery made by a Spanish Admiral Bartholomew de Fontes, "Indeed he would make such a figure in this work as an extract of twenty pages from the well-known Daniel De Foe's Voyage Round the World by a course never sailed before, would when blended with the genuine materals for history gathered from state-papers, or with a collection of authentic records".

    The above extract is taken to prove, that Captain Forster had a high opinion of Mr. Daniel De Foe's abilities as a writer of fiction. And to this opinion every one will readily concur.
                                       THE EDITOR

P.S. Since the above Mr. Shiells, Mr. Paul Whitehead, author of a Poem entitled Manners, a Satire, discovered another work of Mr. De Foe – Memoirs, Travels and

Adventures of a Cavalier, of which a new edition has been lately published by F. Noble, in three volumes, price nine shillings bound.

As will be seen, two things of importance are happening here: Defoe's name is being firmly attached for the first time to some of the novels that his modern readers most prize (e.g. *Moll Flanders* and *Roxana*), and other works (*Memoirs of a Cavalier* and *A New Voyage Round the World*) are, for the first time, being declared not only to be by Defoe, but to be works of fiction. Moreover, for good or evil, Noble's attributions have stuck. That they were made under distinctly dubious circumstances represents the sort of problem that Defoe bibliographers seem doomed to face.

George Chalmers

The first effort at a comprehensive bibliography of Defoe came shortly afterwards. This was a "List of Writings" of Defoe drawn up by the Scottish antiquary George Chalmers in 1790 and included as an appendix to a new edition of his *Life of Daniel De Foe* (first published in 1785). In *The Canonisation of Daniel Defoe* we described the character and activities of the six leading architects of the Defoe "canon", of whom Chalmers was the first. Thus, instead of repeating that account, we shall focus here on the all-important matter of the *transmission* of attributions.

Chalmers's list contained 101 items, of which eighty-one were described as "undoubtedly De Foe's", and a further twenty headed "A List of Books which are supposed to be De Foe's;". (Since his "undoubted" list included separately only thirteen of the forty items contained in the two volumes of Defoe's own authorised *True Collection* of his works, the full total of Chalmers's ascriptions can be said to be 128.)

Chalmers, the first in our chain of bibliographers, had external evidence for some 110 of the items in his list, and attributed the remaining eighteen on grounds of internal evidence alone. The external evidence he depended on, however, was sometimes of a very flimsy kind – for instance that a bookseller had ascribed a work to Defoe; or even, in one or two cases, simply that someone had inscribed a copy with Defoe's name. He had, moreover, some extremely dubious theories about evidence, holding that "every presumption is evidence till the contrary is made apparent", and his career was littered with disastrous enteprises in attribution, of which his championship of Samuel Ireland's preposterous Shakespeare forgeries is merely the most notorious. Thus, though Chalmers's "List of Writings" was a major step forward in Defoe studies and had enormous influence, one is compelled to agree with the verdict of Rodney Baine, who made a close examination of the list and of Chalmers's working papers. "It should now be clear", writes Baine, "that Chalmers' assignment of any particular item to Defoe constitutes in itself no evidence that Defoe wrote it."[12] One is bound to regard any early attribution to Defoe as a piece of external evidence (though of course not necessarily as convincing evidence), and we find it convenient to define "early" as meaning *before* Chalmers.

Walter Wilson

Forty years elapsed between Chalmers's list and Walter Wilson's "Catalogue of De Foe's Works", in the first volume of his *Memoirs of the Life and Times of Daniel De Foe* (1830). Wilson was writing at a time when there was a great deal of (partly topical) interest in Defoe, and a spread of new attributions in booksellers' catalogues and reference works (like Lowndes' *Bibliographer's Manual* and the *Bibliotheca Britannica*). Wilson's list was accordingly much longer than Chalmers's, indeed (at 210 items) nearly twice as long. In his text he mentions some ascriptions suggested by (unnamed) friends, and records acquiring "a knowledge of several of De Foe's pieces, with which I was not previously acquainted" from the collector Machell Stace, who had been planning a catalogue himself but abandoned it on Wilson's behalf.[13]

Wilson dropped eight items from Chalmers's list (and later bibliographers, including Baine, have rejected others as well). Of the eighty-odd items he added to Chalmers, thirty-six are, explicitly or implicitly, firm attributions of his own, the rest being tentative, in degrees varying from strong conviction to almost complete scepticism or a frank admission that he has not in fact seen the work. A few examples will illustrate this (the item number in his list is indicated in brackets). "If not penned by Defoe, it was the production of a kindred writer" (41); "The following work is very much in the manner of Defoe" (87); "This seems to have been written by an Englishman, and perhaps by De Foe" (96). Of no. 140 in his list (*A Letter from a Member of the House of Commons ... Relating to the Bill of Commerce* (1713) we read in the *text* of his biography (iii, p. 331) that, though the work was attributed to Defoe at the time, "there seems [*sic*] no valid reasons" for ascribing it to him.

Wilson, as these examples show, had an extremely relaxed attitude towards attribution. What mattered to him in writing his *Memoirs of the*

---

[12] Rodney M. Baine, "Chalmers' First Bibliography of Daniel Defoe", *Texas Studies in Literature and Language*, 10 (1969), 567.

[13] Machell Stace published anonymously *An Alphabetical Catalogue of an Extensive Collection of the Writings of Daniel De Foe: And of the Different Publications for and against that Very Extraordinary Writer* (London, 1829). It contains some thirty-seven items attributed to Defoe which are not included by Moore.

Life and Times of Daniel De Foe was as much the "times", and in particular
the vicissitudes of the Dissenters, as Defoe himself; and thus it was not
always of major importance to him whether a given work was by Defoe or
not. But – this is the crucial point for our purposes – only someone very
familiar with his enormous and rambling text would have grasped that
fact. His attributions, however tentative, appear without comment in his
"Catalogue of De Foe's Works", and a reader of this naturally takes it that
the ascription can be relied on and is probably supported by some good
external evidence. Wilson moreover increased confusion by starring four
items in his list as "Doubtful". What he actually meant by this, one finds
if one really looks into the matter, is that he was positive in his own mind
that these items were *not* by Defoe, though they were sometimes ascribed
to him. To the uninitiated reader, however, he naturally seems to be
affirming that the rest of the list is secure and not open to doubt.

William Lee

In 1869 William Lee published, in three volumes, *Daniel Defoe: His Life,
and Recently Discovered Writings.* Between his list of Defoe's works and
Wilson's we find a rupture in the chain of transmission of a kind we shall
meet with again. William Lee was exceedingly critical of Wilson's work.
He regarded him as shockingly biased in his conception of Defoe, quite
falsely portraying him as "a bigoted, anti-church, radical Dissenter", and
he condemned Wilson's list as being, like that of Chalmers, "conspicuous
for the absence of all critical acumen, and even ordinary knowledge of
Defoe's stile". Accordingly he rejected thirty items from Wilson's list, as
well as adding sixty-four new ascriptions of his own. Nevertheless – this is
the "rupture" of which we speak – in taking over the remaining 180
attributions from Wilson, it seems all too likely that in some cases he fell
into the same trap as the ordinary reader. Wilson's confusing procedures
led him into imagining that he was more positive in his ascriptions than
was really the case, and that he perhaps knew of evidence which Lee
himself did not.

Lee's *Life* was a major event in the history of Defoe attribution and, in
one particular respect, a source of wide-spreading confusion. This arose
from the fact that Lee was acting both as bibliographer and biographer –
or rather that he was not clear in his own mind, and did not make it clear
to the reader, where the one role ended and the other began. Lee, like
other Defoe bibliographers after him, convinced himself that he had
developed an infallible talent for recognising Defoe's prose style. As he put
it in the Introduction to his *Life* of Defoe, "Long and critical study of a
great author may result in so full an acquaintance, that his writings will be

recognised by the student in a moment, as the voice of a familiar friend".[14] On the strength of this talent he decided that the "Letters Introductory" in *Applebee's Journal* for some six years, starting in in June 1720, were written by Defoe (and not only they, but many news items also). For this he devised a biographical explanation. Defoe been working for the high-flying and seditious Jacobite periodical *Mist's Journal*; but, being a high-minded and patriotic defender of church and state, he had greatly disliked this assignment, and eventually, finding the editor Nathaniel Mist incorrigible, he had broken with him and transferred his services to Applebee.

These contributions to *Applebee's Journal* formed, in Lee's view, a very important and hitherto unsuspected addition to the Defoe canon. He devoted most of the second and third volumes of his *Life* to reprinting them (though even then, as he explains, not including all of them). But, having identified Defoe's hand in these "newly-discovered writings", he was led, as biographer, to draw many consequent conclusions, and indeed to add a whole chapter to Defoe's life story. For John Applebee was the official publisher of the dying speeches and confessions of felons hanged at Tyburn. Since Defoe was on Applebee's staff and payroll, the inference in Lee's eyes was plain: various criminal narratives published by Applebee – a couple associated with the thief Jack Sheppard, and another couple with the thief-catcher Jonathan Wild – must have been written by Defoe. There is evidence Lee had never in fact even seen a copy of two of these pamphlets (Moore nos. **468** and **473**), for in listing them he gives no pagination; so it would seem these attributions owe everything to his *biographical* convictions. Moreover his imagination grew even bolder. He pictured Defoe, as "Applebee's man", being granted privileged access to prisoners in Newgate and conducting interviews with them there, partly on Applebee's behalf, and partly out of a Christian desire to save souls. He even imagined that the elderly novelist, having written his *Narrative of All the Robberies, Escapes etc. of John Sheppard*, had actually appeared at Tyburn, in the guise of "Mr. Applebee", and had mounted the executioner's cart, so that Sheppard, before the assembled multitude, could ceremonially hand him a copy of the pamphlet.

Now, so far as we know, there is not an iota of external evidence that Defoe had any connection with Applebee at all. The entire stirring story is built on Lee's supposed flair for detecting Defoe's hand. This poses awkward problems, evidently, as regards Lee's biography. But it raises equally awkward ones in regard to his bibliography. For what is a later

[14] Lee, *Daniel Defoe*, i, v-vi.

bibliographer to do about these huge swathes of prose, amounting to some 300,000 words, reprinted in volumes 2 and 3 of Lee's *Life*? To our own ears, many of these items do not sound in the least like Defoe. (Would one expect from him a high-Tory defence of "passive obedience" to monarchs? Is it Defoe who writes such bitter words against "Sectaries and Dissenters", blaming them for the spread of the infamous Arian heresy, "as if the Schism they had already made in the Church was not sufficient"? Would he indulge in cheap facetiousness about Moll Flanders, concocting a letter from her supposed niece "Betty Blueskin" telling of her mad passion for Jack Sheppard, lately hanged at Tyburn?)[15] Whether or no he occasionally contributed to *Applebee's Journal* (which is not inconceivable), it is, in our view, totally impossible to accept Lee's blanket ascription to him of this mass of print. Yet, through the inertia that plagues all bibliography, these writings – the *Applebee* writings, as well as the Newgate pamphlets – have survived unquestioned into Moore's list; and many are the articles and books on Defoe or on his period that draw on them.

James Crossley

Soon after the publication of Lee's *Life*, the Manchester book-collector James Crossley, who had already published one or two new Defoe attributions in the pages of *Notes & Queries*, ended a review of the book in that journal with the sensational announcement that "at least fifty more distinct works" not listed by Lee could be "confidently attributed" to Defoe.[16] He did not name them, but at round about the same time he drew up a manuscript list of, in fact, sixty new attributions, a list which eventually came into the possession of the Defoe scholar, George Aitken; and from him into the hands of the first great American authority on Defoe, W.P. Trent. Crossley, the owner of an enormous private library, was held in some awe by both Aitken and Trent, and these new attributions, proposed in oracular manner though without supporting evidence, impressed them greatly. Trent, in a series of articles on Defoe attribution in the New York *Nation* in 1907, wrote:

> To sum up, of the sixty-one [actually sixty] items in Crossley's list, one is now accepted by all, one – "What if the Swedes should come?" – is quite generally accepted, two seem to be mistaken ascriptions, and of the fifty-two (or fifty-three) others that I have examined I find only nine about which I have any real doubt. Of these nine, I suspect that over half are by Defoe, and of the forty-three (or forty-four if there is a duplication of titles) remaining, I am inclined to hold that at least twenty-eight should be accepted

[15] Ibid., iii, 333–35.
[16] J. Crossley, "Defoe's 'Due Preparations for the Plague'", *N & Q*, 4th series, 3 (1869), 402–3.

as readily as almost any entry in Lee's list, and that the fifteen left are so marked by Defoe's characteristics that doubt with regard to them almost partakes of over-scrupulousness. Certainly Crossley, who was of much assistance to Lee, deserves to be remembered as the greatest of all authorities on what is perhaps the most tangled subject in English bibliography.[17]

W.P. Trent

These Crossley attributions helped to swell the vastly-expanded list which W.P. Trent compiled for his article on Defoe in the *Cambridge History of English Literature* in 1912, which was to remain the standard authority for the next forty-eight years. Trent's list comprised 382 items, incorporating fifty-one new attributions from Crossley as well as several suggested by T.J. Wise and H.S. Foxwell. Thus, as will be observed, through Trent's faith in Crossley's intuitions, the practice of attributing items to Defoe purely on internal evidence came to be even more deeply entrenched. Trent, indeed, asserted frankly that in the majority of cases such evidence – from style and content and "favourite phrases" etc. – was all one could look for.

Trent was extremely widely read in early eighteenth-century pamphlet literature, a collector on a grand scale, and probably more versed in the catalogues of the great book-sales and private collections than any subsequent Defoe scholar.[18] He was a tireless worker, amassing an enormous amount of valuable material regarding dates of publication, variant editions and the like, and he could be exceedingly observant when examining anonymous tracts, alert to current allusions and significant resemblances to known Defoe works. The centre of his work in attribution, however, was a system of verbal "tests": a routine of examining works for certain verbal habits and solecisms characteristic of Defoe, like "false concords" (e.g. "neither" followed by "or", or "who" for "whom"), and for favourite phrases and allusions. He repeatedly stressed, it is true, the caution needed in employing such a routine, and admitted that "scarcely a single word or turn of speech is employed by Defoe that cannot be found in the writings of other authors of his period".[19] It was, he said, rather "the way he circulates his verbal money that chiefly helps to reveal our author", and this was a feature "more easily perceived than described". We discussed Trent's working methods at length in the *Canonisation*, and, as we said there, we think his "system" was probably more of a hindrance to him than a help, being unsound logically and often

---

[17] W.P. Trent, "Bibliographical Notes on Defoe – II", *Nation*, 11 July 1907, p. 32.
[18] In his unpublished Bibliography he frequently mentions the David Laing sale and the Doble, Huth and Labouchère collections.
[19] Bibliography, p. 636 (1710).

distracting his attention from the true nature and purpose of the tract he was studying.[20]

Another aspect of Trent's influence also needs to be mentioned. Victorian Defoe scholars were, in the main, champions and admirers, and this was originally the case with Trent. At a certain point in his dealings with Defoe, however (he dated it from his second visit to England on the Defoe quest), his feelings underwent a violent change.[21] He exchanged a faith in Defoe for a notion of him as a "Proteus", a workaholic and a swindler capable of any rascality, and this is the notion of him that he purveys in his highly influential chapter on him in the *Cambridge History of English Literature* in 1912.

> His tracts for the year 1717 alone are sufficiently numerous and discreditable to warrant all that his contemporaries said of him as a mercenary scribbler ... As remarkable, however, as his industry, his versatility, his unscrupulousness and his impudence, is the confidence some modern students, notably Lee, have been able to maintain in him. Many of the tracts belonging to this period have been rejected because of the assumption that Defoe was too virtuous or too dignified to have written them, or that no mortal man could have written so much. It may be safely held that Defoe was capable of writing almost anything, and that few pens have ever filled with greater facility a larger number of sheets.[22]

It is worth noting, in passing, that Trent's naming of the year 1717 is significant. The years 1716 and 1717 are particularly difficult for the Defoe bibliographer, for no longer are the *Review* or Defoe's letters (almost none of which from this period have survived) available as a day-to-day guide to his thoughts and activities, and there are very few really securely attributed works in the light of which to judge doubtful attributions.

At all events, it will be seen what huge implications Trent's new-found scepticism has for bibliography – if behind every banal or fanatical or respectably dull anonymous pamphlet, behind every title-page featuring "An Old Officer" or "Honest Tory" or "Clergy-man of the Church of England", it may be expected to find Defoe lurking. Now, this was the school of thought in which Trent's successor J.R. Moore was brought up. Moore took an altogether more indulgent attitude towards Defoe, though his *Checklist* is such a medley of incompatible and mutually-contradictory items as to take one's breath away, but he would hardly have been such an incorrigible attributor without Trent's example.

[20] See also our article "Defoe, Trent, and the 'Defection'", *RES*, n.s., 44 (1993), 70–76.
[21] See his "Bibliographical Notes on Defoe – I", *Nation*, 6 June 1907.
[22] *Cambridge History of English Literature*, ed. A.W. Ward and A.R. Waller, 14 vols (Cambridge, 1912), ix, 17.

J.R. Moore

This brings us to Moore's *Checklist*, which for some thirty years has been regarded as the ultimate authority in Defoe attribution. It also brings us to another mishap affecting the chain of transmission, perhaps the most serious of all. When Moore began his career as a Defoe scholar, in the 1920s, Trent's *Cambridge History of English Literature* list of 1912 was the standard authority for the canon. Moore was aware that Trent had gone on with his researches after 1912, but he formed the impression that his later work did not amount to much; and, on studying the marginalia in certain volumes which had once belonged to Trent, he decided that his methods were too "impressionistic". Thus when it became known that Trent had in fact compiled a vast unpublished bibliography of Defoe,[23] Moore made no effort to see it. This meant that he was left in ignorance on two important scores. He did not clearly realise that, when Trent's pupil and disciple H.C. Hutchins compiled the "Defoe" entry for the *Cambridge Bibliography of English Literature* (1940), certain new items in it derived from Trent's later researches and the whole entry leaned very heavily on Trent's work. (When he was incapacitated by a stroke in 1927, Trent gave or sold his Bibliography to Hutchins, with the understanding that he would try to find a publisher for it, though he never succeeded in doing so.) Secondly and more importantly Moore was not aware, as he would have been had he seen the Bibliography (for Trent always explained his reasoning in great detail), of how exactly Trent worked, or what his many new attributions in the *Cambridge History* of 1912 had actually been based on. The significance of these facts will be seen when one reads Moore's account of his own development as a bibliographer. Here is how he describes it in the second edition of his *Checklist*:

> After my accidental discovery in 1931 that Defoe wrote "Johnson's" History of the Pyrates,[24] I was content to trace its multifarious relationship to Defoe's other writings. It seemed sufficient to accept the attributions of Trent and Dottin,[25] and to acquaint myself with every work in their lists to be found in the principal libraries or procured through antiquarian booksellers.
>
> That confidence was gradually dispelled as I began to discover unlisted works which were undoubtedly by Defoe (like *A Letter to a Dissenter from his Friend at the Hague* [1688], identified by Defoe himself in *An Appeal to Honour and Justice*), or when entries in the best current lists proved to be impossible for Defoe…
>
> Gradually I was forced to undertake the examination of any publication or

---

[23] The fact was referred to in biographical entries on Trent in various reference works.

[24] See our discussion of **458**, below.

[25] Moore is referring to Paul Dottin, *Daniel De Foe et ses romans*, 3 vols. (Paris and London, 1924).

manuscript between 1680 and 1731 which could reasonably be regarded as Defoe's, and to reconsider every such attribution which had been proposed by responsible writers. *Unless I could offer valid objections against an earlier attribution, I accepted it (at least temporarily) on the assumption that my predecessor might have known of evidence which I had not seen* [our italics].[26]

The crucial sentence here is the last one. Of course, one must allow due weight to the phrase "at least temporarily". Nevertheless one gains a strong impression that Moore fell into the trap we have mentioned before and which has been fatal to so many bibliographers. Finding an item in Trent's *Cambridge History* list he would, for all his growing distrust of Trent, provisionally give it the benefit of the doubt. He would assume it was there for some good reason, involving external evidence; whereas, most probably, Trent had ascribed it purely on internal evidence and the findings of his "tests". Indeed Moore might not always trouble to establish whether it was Trent who first made the ascription; for, whereas Lee had indicated which of his attributions was new, Trent did not follow him in this excellent (and it might be thought, indispensable) practice, any more than Moore himself was to do. Thus Moore inherited much more from Trent than he would have liked to acknowledge or perhaps fully realised. Unknown to himself, he allowed himself to be directed by the very aspect of Trent in which he had so little faith: his powers as a literary critic and skill at recognising Defoe's prose-style.

We then turn to a further and different sort of problem in transmission, connected with Moore's way of launching his attributions. His original plan was to publish a biography of Defoe, including a revised list of his writings as an appendix. For this latter he was using the *CBEL* listing by Hutchins as a basis, and, as he told George Healey in June 1951, he was retaining all Hutchins's items (though he was doubtful about a few of them) except those he was quite sure were not Defoe's. He was, however, adding many new items. On 7 August 1949 he wrote to Healey: "Lately I have run into a great amount of new material – some of the best of it connected with the Peace of Utrecht, the demolition of Dunkirk, trade with France, and so on – the sort of thing that Trent hardly looked into at all. Altogether I have nearer forty than thirty new Defoe titles – works not previously assigned to him but so obviously his that there is no doubt of his authorship when the material is spread out before one." By March 1951 the total of new attributions had reached nearly seventy.

At this point he began lending his list to libraries so that they could recatalogue their Defoe holdings on the strength of it. By January 1952 he

---

[26] Moore, *Checklist*, p. 238.

was able to tell Zoltan Haraszti, the Rare Books Librarian at the Boston Public Library, that the Huntington Library and the Indiana University Library had already revised their catalogues in the light of his checklist; and in September 1952 we find him writing to the Reference Librarian at the Clark Library, asking her to restrict his list to her cataloguers and not to show it to readers, having had unpleasant experiences in the past of scholars stealing his discoveries. On 15 November 1952 he wrote triumphantly to Healey: "Did I ever write you that the British Museum, which had been completely stymied on its Defoe list, has accepted my 21 withdrawals from *CBEL* and my addition of over 100 new titles? That makes the largest single addition to the canon of any writer in English literary history. They will be going to press soon with the new volume of the printed Catalogue, and I am in constant touch with them about details." On 25 September 1958 he told Healey that most of the major libraries were recataloguing, or had recatalogued, their Defoe holdings in the light of his findings; also that the editor of the revised *Dictionary of the Anonymous and Pseudonymous Literature of Great Britain* by Halkett and Laing had assured him that he would "pass up Defoe entirely" and refer readers to Moore's *Checklist*.[27]

In whatever spirit Moore was coming to these arrangements with librarians, their effect is clear and amounted to a prospective self-validation of the *Checklist*. By the time it appeared, the new attributions in the *Checklist* would already be enshrined in library catalogues; and since few users of these catalogues would be likely to question how they had arrived there, it would seem as though these catalogues offered in-dependent corroboration of Moore. The large scope for confusion here can been seen, particularly when one studies the lists Moore was actually sending out to libraries in this run-up period. For, rather naturally, he was inclined to change his mind. In September 1955 he wrote to Healey:

> I have found some new things, but so far perhaps my chief discoveries have been negative. I am realizing, more than before, just how unsatisfactory stylistic tests are, and how much evidence is necessary before one can be CERTAIN of an attribution. I have had to reject two or three of my earlier attributions, good tracts of their kind but simply not Defoe's – the work of some run-of-the-mill Whig pamphleteer who did not have Defoe's special attributes or point of view.

A list of "New Attributions to Defoe" compiled for the Clark Library in late 1953 or thereabouts comprises ninety-four items, of which as many as twenty-one did not survive into the *Checklist*; and there were other similar

[27] For an account of Moore's correspondence with librarians, see Furbank and Owens, *Canonisation*, pp. 117–18.

cases of attributions dropping by the wayside. Indeed in his later years librarians would complain of his insisting they should assign some item to Defoe and then, on revisiting the library a few months later, asking them why on earth they had done so. It is all too probable that attributions that Moore himself later rejected linger on in library catalogues, adding one more knot to the great Defoe tangle.

The manoeuvre that we have been describing is, moreover, merely one aspect of his general approach. It was his habit to describe his discoveries in the field of attribution as though they were not mere hypotheses on his part but matters of impersonal fact, the reader being given no encouragement to pry into the secrets of the scholarly workshop. His instinctive aim, in matters of attribution, was to convey the impression of unquestionable authority. Indeed he succeeded in making it extremely difficult for anyone to question his authority. For in his published *Checklist* – it is a rather extraordinary fact – he gave no indication as to which of his attributions was new. This had the effect, in practice, of shielding the book from informed criticism. It was not possible even for an expert really to judge a book designed in this way, that is to say grapple with its contents in detail, without months or years of labour, and accordingly reviewers largely restricted themselves to generalities. Most gave the book warm praise, though one or two hinting at weaknesses in its methods.[28]

Moore's *Checklist* imposed itself as *the* authority with all the completeness he could have desired. The listing by Maximillian Novak in the *New Cambridge Bibliography of English Literature* of 1971, which came out between the two editions of Moore's *Checklist*, was, in general, based on Moore, though it used an informal code to indicate degrees of probability: "Almost certainly by Defoe", "Probably by Defoe", "Perhaps by Defoe", "Attributed to Defoe by J.R. Moore", "Attributed to Defoe by J.R. Moore, but doubtful", etc. Similarly, Moore's ascriptions to Defoe are treated as authoritative, and their number in his *Checklist* specified, in the *Eighteenth-Century Short Title Catalogue*; and the dependence on them is almost as complete in numerous more specialised catalogues, such as W.A. Speck's edition of F.F. Madan's *Critical Bibliography of Dr. Henry Sacheverell* (Lawrence, Kansas, 1978) and the descriptive checklist of *Anglo-Scottish Tracts, 1701–1714* by W.R. and V.B. McLeod (Lawrence, Kansas, 1979).

We ourselves, as we have made plain, are highly critical of Moore's work and of his whole approach to bibliography. He was unquestionably an indefatigable worker, and it cannot be denied that sometimes he made important discoveries. Certain of his first-time attributions strike one as

---

[28] See, for example, the review by J. Sutherland in *The Library*, 17 (1962), 323–25.

thoroughly convincing, and in one two instances they have later been confirmed by external evidence. There was a case of this recently, when his ascription of *A Memorial to the Nobility of Scotland* (Edinburgh, 1708) received support in a newly-discovered letter from Defoe to Godolphin.[29] On the other hand, among various shortcomings, he had one temperamental defect especially fatal to a bibliographer: he could never admit he was wrong. Confronted with some awkward fact, he would resort to bulldozing tactics, or simply shut his eyes.

We may give an example. In 1965 Henry Snyder published an article suggesting that the famous pamphlet *Advice to the Electors of Great Britain* (1708) (no. **156** in Moore's *Checklist*) was in fact by Arthur Maynwaring and Sarah, Duchess of Marlborough.[30] He argued this on various grounds, but in particular that there actually existed two drafts of it in Maynwaring's hand. (As he remarked in a letter to Moore of 15 February 1966 it was very rare to find the drafts of any political tracts in this period; thus to have two, a rough draft and a finished draft in Maynwaring's own hand, seemed fairly clinching, in the absence of any external evidence connecting the work with Defoe.) Moore, however, was quite unshaken, and he retained the pamphlet in the second (revised) edition of his *Checklist*. In a note he acknowledged Snyder's "very interesting evidence" and conceded that the tract "undoubtedly passed through the hands of that principal agent for the Whigs, and it was apparently edited by him". Nevertheless, he said, it had "marked characteristics of Defoe's style", and "ghost writing for public officials was almost as common in Queen Anne's London as in Washington today".

In *The Canonisation of Daniel Defoe* we gave various other examples of this kind of obstinacy on Moore's part, for instance his resolute refusal, in the face of A.W. Secord's remarkable discoveries, to admit that the real-life Robert Drury could have had anything to do with *Robert Drury's Journal*.[31] There are many more to be found in the present pages. See for instance his refusal to believe that item **421**, *Charity Still a Christian Virtue*, could have been the work of the Revd. William Hendley, at any rate without Defoe's help – despite the fact that Hendley was actually arrested as its author.

[29] See Owens and Furbank, "Defoe as Secret Agent: Three Unpublished Letters", *Scriblerian*, 25 (1993), 145–53.
[30] Henry L. Snyder, "Daniel Defoe, the Duchess of Marlborough, and the *Advice to the Electors of Great Britain*", *HLQ*, 29 (1965–66), 53–62.
[31] See Furbank and Owens, *Canonisation*, pp. 109–13.

Principles and Methods in Author-Attribution

The chequered history of the Defoe "canon" raises many questions about the theory of author-attribution. We devoted a chapter of our book to the subject, and we will repeat a few points from it here. We suggest that, for an authorial canon to be soundly based, three basic rules need to have been observed:

1. In arguing for a new attribution, one should not "forge chains" of attribution, that is to say base any part of one's argument on some earlier merely tentative or plausible attribution, but should draw solely upon works indisputably by the author in question.
2. If adding a new ascription, one should always explain one's reasons.
3. One should not regard the fact that a new ascription seems plausible – i.e. compatible with the author's known style or interests etc. – as in itself sufficient reason for adding the work to the canon; nor should one be tempted to add a work to the canon "provisionally", i.e. until some better candidate for authorship offers himself. (The reason, in both cases, is that the addition of a work to the canon causes a qualitative change in its status, transforming the way in which later scholars are expected to regard it. It is infinitely harder to get a work *out* of the canon than to put it there in the first place.)

On the vexed question of the relative rights of external versus internal evidence, we hold that external evidence should be granted, not so much greater weight, as a *logical* priority over internal. The most natural situation in author-attribution is when some piece of external evidence, possibly quite slight, raises the suspicion that a work may be by a given author – in which case internal evidence may exercise great weight and may even be conclusive. For a twentieth-century bibliographer to ascribe a work to Defoe on internal evidence alone seems to us a rash business, only justified in very exceptional cases. Further, an ascription based on internal evidence alone can never claim to be more than "probable". (We shall divide the items in our *CBEL3* list into two categories, "By Defoe" and "Probably by Defoe".)

It is common for bibliographers to ascribe a work to an author on the basis of an accumulation of parallels with other, known, works of his, but in our view this is open to various dangers. Low-quality parallels, that is to say ones so vague as to possess no real distinctiveness, are really of no significance at all and do not gain any by mere accumulation. Nor, in the case of higher quality parallels, are there any mathematical rules for deciding how they "add up"; any judgement on this has to be purely personal and impressionistic. Further, to repeat an earlier point, parallels drawn from works that are themselves only "probable" not "certain" attributions are worthless.

Much of the work in attribution done by Lee, Trent and Moore is based on "favourite phrases" and "favourite allusions" of Defoe's. We are inclined to think that dependence on "favourite phrases" has led them astray and is altogether unsatisfactory. First, because it is illogical, since – as Trent in fact admitted – none of the phrases that he, or the others, chose to regard as "favourites" of Defoe's were peculiar to him, nor is there any way of being certain that some other writer did not use them just as liberally. Secondly, because looking for "favourite phrases", as a matter of routine, can lead to lazy reading and the search for a short-cut in attribution.

The case seems to us different with "favourite allusions". Among the allusions and anecdotes often found in Defoe, some seem sufficiently striking and idiosyncratic to carry, anyway potentially, a certain weight in attribution – though remembering that it cannot be assumed they were his private and exclusive property. How much weight they should carry, or in what proportion it is increased by the presence of two or three such "favourite allusions" in the same work, is a different question, to which no general answer can be made; but it would seem perverse to disregard them altogether. We are thinking, for instance, of Defoe's often repeated story of the soldiers in Barcelona who insisted on eating grapes and told their officer that they were Englishmen and ought to be at liberty to kill themselves if they chose to. Or his frequent allusions to blowing up one man's house to save a burning street; to Caesar's maxim, never to despise an enemy; to the Pope who exclaimed "How much profit we make from this fable of Christ!"; to Gustavus Adolphus and his "iron-faced" Swedes; to the Oliverian captain who told his men, "The day's our own, the enemy have started to blaspheme"; to Lycurgus's making no law against parricide, considering it too terrible to imagine, etc.

We think that literary value can play a part in attribution, but mainly a negative one. Defoe no doubt sometimes wrote badly, but it is safe to assume that he was not capable of certain *kinds* of badness, as of certain *kinds* of excellence. The converse proposition, that only Defoe ("Who but Defoe?") possessed the talent to write such-and-such a passage, strikes us much less safe, indeed as illusory, as does the conviction, shared by Lee, Trent and Moore, that one can develop an infallible knack for recognising Defoe's prose-style.

Finally, it is sometimes suggested that the best approach to Defoe-attribution problems might be "stylometry" – that is to say, the statistical analysis of verbal habits. The basic assumption of stylometry is that authors have distinguishable habits in the rate at which they perform operations common to all users of language (as it might be, beginning a sentence with the word "the"), and that, given a large enough sample, it ought to be possible to identify such habits by statistical analysis, aided by the computer. From a reading of the work of A.Q. Morton, M.W.A. Smith and Anthony Kenny, our own opinion, for what it is worth, is that there could potentially be something in the theory in cases where there are only a few, known candidates for authorship (as is true with Elizabethan drama), but that it has no way of coping, as would be necessary in Defoe-attribution, with the case of "author X against the world" – that is to say, when there is no limit to the number of possible authors. In other words the claim, sometimes made by A.Q. Morton and others, that authors have a statistical "fingerprint" distinguishing them from all comers, appears to us unfounded.[32]

[32] For further discussion see Furbank and Owens, *Canonisation*, pp. 176–183, and our article "Dangerous Relations", *Scriblerian*, 23 (1991), 242–44.

DE-ATTRIBUTIONS

4 [Pamphlet of 1687 against Addresses to James II]

ATTRIBUTION: Moore.

Moore supposes that such a tract must exist because of Defoe's statement in the *Review*, 24 November 1711, that as a young man he had earned the "Reproaches" of his Dissenting friends when he "protested openly" against addresses of thanks to James II for his first Declaration of Indulgence. However, Defoe goes on to say, "I had their Anger again, when, in print, I oppos'd at the utmost hazard, the taking off the Penal Laws and Test... ", thus implying that his earlier protest had not been published

6 Reflections upon the Late Great Revolution

London: Printed for Ric. Chiswell, 1689

ATTRIBUTION: Hutchins; Moore (as "Mistakenly attributed in *State Tracts* to a Mr. Eyres"), Novak (as "Probably by Defoe").

A pious tract, proving by a long sucession of biblical texts that monarchy is not the only form of government blessed by God and that in the past the People have often had a say in the election of kings. It ends with a devout thanksgiving for the "deliverance" by William III. The author, who describes himself as "a Lay-Hand in the Country", speaks as a believer in the divine appointment of bishops.

It is difficult to surmise what could have prompted this attribution, and why the external evidence ascribing the tract to "Mr. Eyres" should have been dismissed. Moore was evidently uneasy about it, since in his *Daniel Defoe: Citizen of the Modern World* (Chicago, 1958), p. 72, he cites "this old-fashioned tract" as evidence that Defoe had not yet mastered his trade as a political writer, and in another article admitted that "it read more like the laboured scriptural argument of a dissenting parson than anything by a propagandist for William". See "Daniel Defoe: King William's Pamphleteer and Intelligence Agent", *HLQ*, 34 (1971), 256.

7 The Advantages of the Present Settlement

London: Printed for Ric. Chiswell, 1689

ATTRIBUTION: Moore (who describes it as "Mistakenly attributed in *State Tracts* to P.A., D.D."); Novak (as "Probably by Defoe").

A statement of the Whig position, written as by a humble and obscure member of the Church of England in the country, reflecting on the great dangers of popery and tyranny lately escaped, thanks to William III, and on the folly of those who remain discontented. It is written in an ample and orotund style not at all suggestive of Defoe. Moore does not explain his reasons for rejecting the attribution to "P.A., D.D.", who would' appear to be Pierre Allix (1641–1717), a French Protestant minister who took refuge in England as a result of the revocation of the Edict of Nantes. He wrote numerous works of theology and church history and received doctorates in divinity from Oxford and Cambridge. Six other tracts are also given to him in *State Tracts*.

8 An Account of the Late Horrid Conspiracy

London: Printed for J. Humphrys, 1691

ATTRIBUTION: Moore; Novak (as "Probably by Defoe").

A stop-press account of Lord Preston's Jacobite conspiracy and its discovery and of his and his associates' trial at the Old Bailey in January. Moore gives no reason for attributing this to Defoe, and it is hard to guess why he should have done so. The fact that Defoe dealt with the Preston affair in his poem *A New Discovery of an Old Intreague* (1691) clearly offers no particular support to the ascription.

8a A Compleat History of the Late Revolution

London: Printed for Samuel Clement, 1691

ATTRIBUTION: Moore, at the suggestion of F. Bastian (as "Sometimes mistakenly assigned to Guy Miege").

A history of the rise of popery and tyranny in England under Charles II and James and of its overthrow by William III. The "warming-pan" affair is recorded in great detail.

Guy Miege (1644–1718?) included this in a list of his own writings in his tract *Utrum Horum?* (1705) – see Frank Bastian, "Defoe and Guy Miege", *N & Q*, n.s., 16 (1969), 103 – and *pace* Bastian, who supposes some kind of collaboration between Miege and Defoe, it is hard to see any good reason for disbelieving Miege's claim.

10a Reflections upon the Late Horrid Conspiracy ... to Murther His Majesty in Flanders

London: Printed for Richard Baldwin, 1692

ATTRIBUTION: Moore.

An account of the plot to assassinate King William which came to light in the spring of 1692. Although the would-be assassin Grandval, in his confession, only implicated his immediate superior, the French Secretary of State Barbesieux, the author argues that Louis XIV must have been privy to the plot, and he contrasts this infamy with the shining integrity of William, whom Providence appears to have decided to protect.

Moore announced his attribution in "Daniel Defoe: King William's Pamphleteer and Intelligence Agent", *HLQ*, 34 (1971), 251–60, describing it as "the first known publication" in which Defoe was acting as "a trusted agent of the King". He offered no evidence in support of the ascription, and his case for such an early association of Defoe with William appears to be based on a series of similarly arbitrary attributions – a view shared by J.A. Downie in "Defoe's Early Writings" (forthcoming in *RES*). Nothing in the style or matter particularly suggests Defoe's authorship.

10b A Dialogue betwixt Whig and Tory

[London]: Printed in the Year 1693

ATTRIBUTION: Moore; Novak (as "Probably by Defoe").

An inflammatory tract, advising the King what to do to rescue the country from its present deplorable state (he should dismiss disloyal Tory Ministers, should become an entire Englishman, should not attempt to influence elections, etc.), and staging a dialogue between a Whig and a Tory, in which the Tory levels all the standard charges against the Whigs but frankly declares himself an opportunist and pragmatist, who will not "die a martyr for any Monarch" (p. 8). The Whig says he and his friends will welcome back any penitent Tory prodigals and admits there are some "knaves" and renegades within his own party.

The tract was attributed to "B.O. Esq." when re-issued in *A Collection of State Tracts* in 1706. J.A. Downie, in "Ben Overton: An Alternative Author of *A Dialogue betwixt Whig and Tory*", *PBSA*, 70 (1976), 263–71, convincingly interprets the tract as Sunderlandite propaganda related to the ministerial changes in 1693 and interprets "B.O. Esq." as signifying the Whig pamphleteer Ben Overton, whom he regards as the most likely author.

Moore seems to have been led to this late attribution by the fact that the pamphlet was re-issued in 1710 by Sarah Popping, who published several other works which he also came to believe were by Defoe, including the *Observator* from 19 July to early October 1710. His theory about Popping, which turns on references to some of these newly-attributed works in the *Observator*, appears somewhat circular. Previously, he had frequently referred in his letters to *A Dialogue betwixt Whig and Tory* as a tract he had once attributed to Defoe but now thought more likely to be by Oldmixon.

*12 An Answer to the Late K[ing] James's Last Declaration

London: Printed for Richard Baldwin, 1693

ATTRIBUTION: Moore.

A paragraph by paragraph reply to King James II's famous Declaration of April 1693, arguing forcefully that no statement in it can be trusted in view of James's record of tyranny and deception. The author of a rejoinder, *A Reply to the Answer Doctor Welwood has Made to King James's Declaration* (1694), clearly assigns it to James Welwood, a prominent Whig propagandist and author of an earlier *Answer to the Late King James's*

Declaration (1689), and there seems no reason to question this contemporary ascription. Moore argues against Welwood's authorship on the grounds that Welwood always signed his tracts and claims that "Internal evidence is strongly in favor of an attribution to Defoe", adding in the Second Supplement to the *Checklist* (p. 242) that the mistaken attribution to Welwood shows that the Jacobite author of the *Reply* was "out of touch with affairs in London". In a letter to Frank Bastian 19 August 1970 he elaborates on the stylistic unlikelihood of the tract's being by Welwood, "a learned medical man who wrote like a courtier in a leisurely style and long involved sentences", but we ourselves can detect no marked difference in style between the earlier and the later *Answer*.

13 The Englishman's Choice, and True Interest

London: Printed in the Year 1694

ATTRIBUTION: Lee; Hutchins, Moore, Novak (as "Almost certainly by Defoe").

A rather repetitive attack on the enemies of King William's military policy and of his great services to the Protestant cause: time-serving traitors who would want to deny him a standing army and begrudge the just debt to the Dutch for military aid, men who raise the bogey of "Commonwealth" doctrines and are vindictive towards French Protestant refugees.

Lee does not explain why he attributes this tract to Defoe, and the hectoring rhetoric (e.g. on p. 28: "God be thanked, we have a Prince who will not quit His possession without bloody Shirts") does not suggest him.

13a Some Seasonable Queries on the Third Head, viz. a General Naturalization

[London, 1697]

ATTRIBUTION: Moore; Novak (as "Probably by Defoe").

This four-page pamphlet, taking the form of eighteen "queries" and a conclusion, is in support of a Bill to naturalise foreigners which was before Parliament in February 1697. It argues strongly that the Act will help increase the population, which in turn would contribute to national prosperity. Earlier generations of immigrants, such as the Huguenots, taught valuable new manufacturing skills, and nothing could be a "greater mortification" to Louis XIV than to see England strengthened by "a considerable Accession of zealous Protestants".

In "Defoe's *Some Seasonable Queries*: A Chapter Concerning the

Humanities", *Newberry Library Bulletin*, 6 (1965), 179–86, Moore argues that "any serious doubt concerning Defoe's authorship disappeared" when it became clear that the pamphlet was addressed to Parliament, in a way especially favoured by Defoe, i.e. given to M.P.s free of charge. This strikes one as a distinctly flimsy argument.

He also finds verbal parallels with *The Englishman's Choice* (1694) (**13**, *q.v.*) and *A Continuation of Letters Written by a Turkish Spy* (1718) (Moore, **406**). However, there is little reason to regard the first of these as being by Defoe, and the parallel with the second is quite negligible. In addition, he cites "parallels" in ideas, in particular the view that economic prosperity is linked to high population. This is certainly a favourite theme of Defoe's (see for instance the *Review* for 24 and 26 February and 1 and 15 March 1709, in connection with a later Bill to naturalise foreign Protestants), but, as Peter Earle points out in *The World of Defoe* (1976), p. 147, "Defoe's desire to increase England's population was common to nearly all the writers of his day".

Moore fails to mention one or two apparent anomalies. The argument in the tract about the advantage of more seamen for the navy conflicts somewhat with the reasoning in Defoe's *Essay upon Projects* of the same year, which asserts that there is no shortage of seamen in England, it is merely that, as things are, they find better pay and conditions in merchant ships. Equally, the author's belief that Ireland presents no economic threat to England does not really square with Defoe's insistence on the correctness of the decision to prohibit exports of Irish woollen manufactures (see *Review*, 24 April 1705).

17a Some Queries concerning the Disbanding of the Army ... Which May Serve for an Answer to Mr. A, B, C, D, E, F, G's Argument

[London]: Printed in the Year 1698

ATTRIBUTION: Moore.

The Dedication to the famous pamphlet by John Trenchard and Walter Moyle, *An Argument Shewing that a Standing Army is Inconsistent with a Free Government* (1697), was signed "Mr. A, B, C, D, E, F, G", and the present tract, as the title suggests, is a series of queries on their arguments for disbanding William III's army. Is not the French King a great and imminent danger? Do we not have to choose a standing army as the lesser of two evils? Is a militia a match for a disciplined opponent? Could not an army be useful in peace-time, e.g. for mending the roads? Would not keeping a large fleet (necessary if we have no land forces) entail the use of press-gangs to force seamen out of merchant ships, thus endangering trade?

Moore's case for attributing this to Defoe is presented in his "Defoe Acquisitions at the Huntington Library", *HLQ*, 28 (1964), 45–57, and consists of four points: (1) *Some Queries*, like *Some Reflections on a Pamphlet Lately Publish'd* of the previous year (a work safely to be attributed to Defoe since it is signed "D.F."), ridicules Trenchard and Moyle's use of "A, B, C, D, E, F, G" as a signature; (2) like *Some Reflections*, *Some Queries* jeers at a statement by Trenchard and Moyle that "what happened yesterday, will come to pass again"; (3) *Some Queries*, though brief, "has many characteristic Defoe idioms and many of Defoe's favourite ideas, such as the appeal to any person who knows what armies are" (p. 5), the proposal to encourage inland trade and to employ soldiers in guarding the highways (p. 7), and the fear that pressing seamen for the navy would cripple merchant shipping (p. 7); (4) "Most of all, the presentation of an argument by propounding queries, was...a favourite with Defoe". Against these it may be objected that neither tract is "ridiculing" the use of the seven initials; the remark "what happened yesterday, etc." is explicitly and repeatedly mocked in *Some Reflections*, but this is hardly the case in *Some Queries*; Moore does not specify the parallels he has in mind for the "favourite ideas" he cites; and, finally, the use of "Queries" as a polemical device can hardly be regarded as Defoe's private property. His case for ascribing the work to Defoe thus appears insufficient.

19a The Case of Disbanding the Army at Present, Briefly and Impartially Consider'd

[London]: Published by John Nutt, 1698

ATTRIBUTION: Moore.

A simple and straightforward statement of the need for a standing army in the current situation, with Louis XIV eager to enslave all Europe. It reminds those who say that a fleet would be enough protection that King William, unlike Louis XIV, needs parliamentary approval before employing a fleet; and it points out that a militia, to be of use, would need to be directed by the King just as much as a standing army.

Moore, in his *Checklist* (pp. 255–56), remarks that this is "a characteristic work by Defoe, developing the same ideas, with many of the same idioms", as *Some Reflections on a Pamphlet Lately Publish'd* (1697) (signed "D.F."), *An Argument Shewing, that a Standing Army, with Consent of Parliament, is not*

Inconsistent a with a Free Government (1698) (in Defoe's *True Collection*) and *A Brief Reply to the History of Standing Armies in England* (1698) (ditto). However, a reading of these three works hardly bears this out; and in the absence of external evidence and any really compelling internal evidence the ascription must be regarded as unproven.

21 The Interests of the Several Princes and States of Europe Consider'd, with Respect to the Succession of the Crown of Spain

London: Printed in the Year 1698

ATTRIBUTION: Trent (Bibliography); Hutchins, Moore, Novak.

A detailed and knowledgeable analysis of the diplomatic problem which would face Europe on the death of Charles II of Spain and of the various dynastic claims to his throne. It stresses the threat to the balance of power if France were to be united with Spain, and in particular the danger to English and Dutch trade. "It must be the Interest of all the Princes of *Europe* to join their Forces with the utmost vigour, and endeavour to prevent it" (p. 29).

Trent acknowledges a lack of "special idiosyncratic touches" marking this as by Defoe but is inclined to attribute it to him on the strength of its knowledgeability about Spanish trade. "The writer of the pamphlet knew a good deal about Spanish trade, which is what we should expect of Defoe who in his early years held some commercial position in that country."

The inadequacy of Trent's reasoning as the basis for a positive attribution to Defoe is obvious. One would not rule out the possibility of his authorship, but no good case for it has so far been made.

34 The Apparent Danger of an Invasion, Briefly Represented in a Letter to a Minister of State. By a Kentish Gentleman

London: Printed and Sold by A. Baldwin, 1701

ATTRIBUTION: Moore (as "Very probably, not certainly, Defoe's"); Novak (as "Perhaps by Defoe").

An alarmist pamphlet, dated "14 February", pointing out the ease with which, in the present defenceless state of England and with the number of traitors in its midst, the French could invade it and ravage Kent and Sussex, as they had the Palatinate.

In "Defoe Acquisitions at the Huntington Library", *HLQ*, 28 (1964),

45–57, Moore speaks of "additional evidence" leaving "no room to doubt that [this] is a very characteristic work by Defoe'. He does not specify what this "additional evidence" is, and one can only surmise that he may be referring to a passage on p. 2 which speaks of "the folly of a few true Born *Englishman* [*sic*]" who would not listen to the advice of William, a "very worthy Gentleman & true *Englishman* too", and would not allow a standing army "for fear, I suppose, That Englishmen should Englishmen subdue".

Defoe's known political writings in the momentous year following the death of Charles II of Spain are framed at the level of high politics and the "balance of power" and, in the case of *The Present State of Jacobitism* (Moore, **38**) and *Reasons against a War* (Moore, **39**), argue in statesmanlike tones for a pacific foreign policy. *Legion's Memorial* (Moore, **35**), which there is reason to think is his, is also a very cogent piece of political thinking, intended to be of use to William III. Thus it is hard to imagine Defoe composing this scaremongering tract, which it would be more natural to suppose was by one of the "Kentish Gentlemen" responsible for the Kentish petition.

46 Good Advice to the Ladies ... By the Author of *The True-Born Englishman*

London: Printed in the Year 1702

ATTRIBUTION: Lee; Trent (*CHEL*), Hutchins, Moore, Novak (as "Probably by Defoe").

A satire in heroic couplets on the vices of modern husbands, addressed to *Lesbia* as an encouragement not to marry.

Defoe appears to disown this poem in the *Little Review* for 20 June 1705. A.M. Wilkinson, in "*Good Advice to the Ladies*: A Note on Daniel Defoe", *N & Q*, 195 (1950), 273–75, argues that the wording of the denial is deliberately ambiguous, and Lee (p. 63) makes the related point that Defoe was only complaining of being pirated. However, as against Wilkinson, it would be reasonable to take Defoe, when he says he "writes nothing but what he publickly owns", as meaning by this signing with his initials and not merely employing the sobriquet "The Author of the True-Born Englishman". Lee's reading also does not quite stand up, since Defoe is complaining of printers pirating *fragments* of larger works. But the half-joking tone of Defoe's denial leaves it uncertain whether it is meant to be believed.

Toland, in an undated fictitious letter "My Aversion and Inclination:

In a Letter to Mrs. D***" (*A Collection of Several Pieces of Mr. John Toland* [1726], ii, 357–64), could be thought to be alluding to this poem and to Defoe as its author, when he tells "Mrs D***" that the rumour that "Dame SCRAGG" is in love with himself has been confirmed by "one, who has an unlucky talent at writing merry Ballads and waggish Lampoons". Such a talent, he says, "is enough, I confess, to beget a terrible idea of that wight, in the breasts of all those Ladies who blush as soon as they hear him nam'd; which are the foolish, the frail, and the fickle, the tattlers, the dawbers, the modish, and the coquets, to all which I know her Ladyship to be a perfect stranger. Those characters will reach nevertheless to a world of other women; which makes me wonder, that the adventurous Poet does not put all the timorous fair under contribution; which wou'd be a surer way of enriching himself than by dabbling (as he does now) in Politics, or by drudging (as he did before) in Trade." It has to be objected, though, that *Good Advice* is a satire on husbands, not on wives.

Thus the case for Defoe's authorship is somewhat tenuous, and it needs to be remembered that many poems were saddled illegitimately upon "The Author of *The True-Born Englishman*". Accordingly one is thrown back on one's stylistic intuitions, which in our case are rather against the poem's being by Defoe. For one thing, the run of the verses, and the particular way of handling enjambment, do not sound right for him.

53 King William's Affection to the Church of England Examin'd

London: Printed in the Year 1703

ATTRIBUTION: Wilson; Lee, Trent (*CHEL*), Hutchins, Moore, Novak.

A heavily ironical pamphlet, written as by a high-flyer impatient at Whig allegations of ingratitude to the late King William. In setting out "to prove that the Church of *England* was in no great or apparent danger from the mistakes of King *James*'s Government, nor so mightily deliver'd by K. *W*–'s" (p. 3), the author actually reveals the opposite to the reader, who is presented with overwhelming evidence that William had the good of the Church always at heart and indeed died "in the Communion of it". In the final few pages the irony is abandoned completely, giving way to an outright condemnation of those who besmirch William's memory.

Since at the very moment of this tract's publication (late March) Defoe was in hiding from the authorities, having been condemned in his absence for *The Shortest Way*, it seems unlikely that he would have risked publishing another ironical impersonation of a high-flyer, one, moreover, which takes the opportunity to have a swipe at erstwhile supporters of James now back in office (p. 6). There is nothing in the tract which specifically suggests Defoe's authorship; on the contrary, a passage on p. 23 which seems, more or less unironically, to speak of the Dissenters' manner of worship as "slovenly" and "rude" would be hard to reconcile with him.

It should be noted that Wilson's original attribution was characteristically tentative: "If not penned by De Foe, it was the production of a kindred writer" (ii, 96), and according to Trent the tract has sometimes been attributed to Lord Somers. In the absence of any real evidence, the authority of a succession of Defoe bibliographers seems insufficient to justify its retention in the canon.

54 A Collection of the Writings of the Author of *The True-Born English-Man*

London: Printed in the Year 1703

ATTRIBUTION: Moore (in *Defoe in the Pillory*); Novak (as "Collected by Defoe, though he claimed it was pirated").

A collection of thirteen items published by John How on 17 April 1703, while Defoe was in hiding from the authorities for *The Shortest Way*. In his Preface to a volume entitled *A True Collection of the Writings of the Author of The True Born English-Man*, published 22 July 1703, Defoe vehemently repudiated the *Collection* as a piracy, complaining that his works had been hideously mangled, and that it had been "a most unaccountable piece of Boldness" for the "Piratical Printer" to have reprinted *The Shortest Way* "while I lay under the publick Resentment for the same Fact". The *True Collection*, which appeared with an engraved portrait of Defoe, dropped two of the works in the *Collection*, and added eleven more.

Bibliographers before Moore accepted Defoe's claims of piracy, and treated the *Collection* as spurious. However, in his *Defoe in the Pillory and Other Studies* (Bloomington, Indiana, 1939), Moore argued that all the works in the *Collection* were by Defoe, and demonstrated furthermore that for certain works the printer of the *True Collection* had used the *Collection* as his copy-text. This prompted Moore to the conclusion that Defoe himself must have been responsible for the *Collection*.

So far as one can see, this is an implausible and quite unnecessary speculation on Moore's part. A more simple explanation of the facts would be that, discovering that How had produced a pirated edition of some of his writings, Defoe, by this time in prison, decided to produce his own

"True" collection, and for convenience he resolved, at least initially, to use the How version as a copy-text; but having done so with a few of the works, he found they needed too much correcting, so, for the rest, he made use of the original editions in pamphlet form. This indeed seems to be, roughly speaking, what he is implying in the Preface to the *True Collection*: "I set about Correcting the Mistakes of the Book they have Publish'd, till I came to above three hundred Errors; and then being weary of Amendment, I resolv'd to disabuse the World with a corrected Copy." (For what reason would he have been correcting the How text, except to use it as a copy-text?)

Other reasons advanced by Moore in support of his theory that Defoe was behind the *Collection* are no more convincing. He argues (1) that for prudential reasons Defoe could not risk being involved with a *Collection* including *The Shortest Way*, and so had elaborately to disown it; (2) that the *Collection* was "an intelligently made selection of Defoe's latest and best tracts", unlike the *True Collection* which included older and less well-known material; (3) that it is strange if the *Collection* really was a piracy that it did not highlight as a selling point the still-topical *Shortest Way*, rather than giving prominence to *The True-Born Englishman*, which had faded from public attention; we know that Defoe was proud of his poem, and therefore it is more likely that he would have named it in the title.

These reasons seem extraordinarily flimsy, and no answer to the implausibility of Defoe's sponsoring a botched and ill-printed collection of his writings in rivalry with a handsome and much larger one, nor to the question why he would have included two works in this earlier collection which he dropped from the later one. Whether he was in fact the author of these two works is a different question. Our own view is that he probably was. (It is worth noting that a comment by Moore to the effect that Defoe was making a false claim in asserting that the *True Collection* contained "above double the number of Tracts that were printed in the said sham Collection" is somewhat unfair, since if one deducts the two omitted tracts from the calculation, the *True Collection* can be said to contain exactly double the number of works included in the *Collection*, i.e. twenty-two as opposed to eleven.) If it is accepted that the How *Collection* was a piracy, and that Defoe did not in any way authorise its publication, it does not seem right to include it in a list of his works.

62 The Case of Dissenters as Affected by the Late Bill Proposed in Parliament for Preventing Occasional Conformity. By a Gentleman

London: Printed and Sold by A. Baldwin, 1703

ATTRIBUTION: Trent (*Nation*) ("Everything makes for Defoe's authorship, but there seems to be need for a greater abundance of characteristic features"); Hutchins, Moore, Novak.

A sanctimonious and prosy tract, stuffed with "thereof"s, "unto"s, "peradventure"s, etc., arguing that the recent Occasional Conformity Bill, though well intentioned, could have led, if it had been passed, to a revival of old animosities. Since the purpose was to encourage Anglican orthodoxy, not to create prejudice against Dissent, would it not have been more logical to increase the required number of attendances at Anglican communion to *four*? The author can imagine excellent motives for Occasional Conformity, as "an Expression of Charity to others" (p. 9). (The rest of the tract is concerned with the Test and Corporation Acts.)

The style does not remotely suggest Defoe, and the views about Occasional Conformity are utterly different from the ones in tracts known to be his – e.g. *An Enquiry into Occasional Conformity, Shewing that the Dissenters are No Way Concern'd in It* (1702) (Moore, **48**), which discusses the same Bill. A most implausible attribution.

73 Moderation Maintain'd ... in a Sermon Preached the Thirty-First of January at Aldgate Church, by White Kennet

London: Printed in the Year 1704

ATTRIBUTION: Trent (*Nation*); Hutchins, Moore, Novak.

A defence, published on 27 March 1704, of White Kennet's notorious sermon critical of Charles I (delivered on the day after the anniversary of Charles's execution and published as *A Compassionate Enquiry into the Causes of the Civil War*) against an attack on it entitled *The Remarks on a Sermon, Preached January the 31st*, 1703/4, sometimes attributed to Henry Gandy. It praises Kennet's moderate stance and defends his use of the term "civil war" instead of "rebellion". The Preface is signed "D.F.'

In the *London Post* for 27–29 March, and for several subsequent issues, *Moderation Maintain'd* was advertised as "By D.F.", and to be "Sold by the Publisher of this Paper", i.e. Benjamin Harris. In his *Review* for 4 April

1704, Defoe arraigned Harris before the Scandal Club for "putting D.F. as the Author of a certain Book of his own making, the Person he own'd to be meant, having declared he knew nothing of it". Harris, in defence, is made to plead "the Custom of his Trade to put any Name to a Book, when he thinks it will sell the better", etc. Presumably in response to this, Harris dropped the attribution to "D.F." from his advertisements for the tract in the *London Post* after the issue for 12–14 April.

The tract does not sound like Defoe, being excessively sanctimonious in tone and indulging in dreadfully flat-footed irony over the author's description of himself as a "Gentleman". Also, it is written as if by a Churchman; hence it would seem illogical for Defoe to sign it with his initials, considering that he was about the most famous Dissenter in England at the time. This, together with the significant fact that Harris amended the wording of his advertisements, makes it reasonable to accept Defoe's repudiation of the work.

74 Legion's Humble Address to the Lords

[London, 1704]

ATTRIBUTION: Lee; Moore, Novak.

On 28 March 1704 the House of Lords voted in favour of an appeal against disfranchisement by Ashby, an Aylesbury cobbler. The present pamphlet, following closely on this event, is a petition to the Lords (presented sometime before 3 April, when the Queen closed the current session of Parliament), saying that the "Distressed People of *England*" beg the Lords for redress against such constitutional encroachments as Ashby was victim of, and other threats to liberty and the Protestant succession attempted by the House of Commons. It ends "*Our Name is* Million, *and We are more*".

The publication of this subversive tract brought in its wake a series of arrests and official interrogations, though Defoe, who was strongly suspected of its authorship, seems never to have been formally charged with it. There can be no doubt that he was deeply involved in it, in conjunction with a certain John Pierce, and there is a quantity of external evidence connecting both with the tract. The story is extremely complicated, however, and, in Defoe's case, is hard to disentangle from the history of his *Master Mercury* and the satirical poem "The Address", published at much the same time as *Legion's Humble Address*. Some aspects of the story are dealt with by Pat Rogers in "An Eighteenth-Century Alarm: Defoe, Sir Justinian Isham and the Secretaries of State", *Northamptonshire Past and Present*, 4 (1966–71), 383–87, and we are ourselves planning an article on the subject. For present purposes it seems best simply to list the external evidence of authorship, from which it will appear that, if anything, the weight of evidence is in favour of Pierce, rather than Defoe, as the actual author. The career of John Pierce, mentioned several times by Defoe as his agent in Scotland (see *Letters*, p. 163), evidently needs further investigation.

The Evidence. On 25 May 1704 the Queen offered a reward for discovery of the author and printer of *Legion's Humble Address*. Defoe, in the *Review* for 3 June, appealed jocularly to the "Scandal Club" against a "very Scandalous Letter", which quoted a certain person as accusing him of authorship of *Legion's Humble Address*. He challenged the world to prove the accusation, and, to scotch rumours that he was fled from justice, said that he had thoughts of exposing himself to view at stated hours for two pence a time. On 8 June, Narcissus Luttrell reported that "Mr. James Rawlins, a printer, and one Mr. Peirce, an exchange broker, abscond; the first being accused for printing Legion's Address to the Lords, and the last for handing it to the presse". On 14 June an informer wrote to Harley that "if Dan Foe be the supposed author of the libel titled 'Legion's Address to the Lords'" he was to be found at "Captain Roger's" in Canterbury. On 19 June the Secretary of State Sir Charles Hedges received information that the printer Rawlins had been arrested near Market Harborough and had confessed to getting Robert Clare his journeyman to print *Legion's Humble Address*, for which "one Pierce a Broker, formerly a Silkman" paid him about forty shillings, and to going to Newcastle in the company of Pierce. (When Rawlins was arrested, he had a copy of the offending tract in his pocket, but he claimed that it was not one of those he had printed himself, and that he had bought it in Newcastle.) On 5 July an informer told Harley that Toland was in England; Defoe was writing "a History of Superstition"; and John Pierce, "reputed author of the *Million Letter*", was also in England, though the informer did not know where. On 27 September Nathaniel Sammon, "a tool of De Foe's", was arrested by warrant from Hedges, as "disperser of the Address", and he admitted receiving a bundle of papers from "one John Pearse" and giving them to the bookseller Lintot (also later asking Lintot if he wanted more). He would not reveal the names of any accomplices. A newsletter dated London, 10 February 1705 (*Historical Manuscripts Commission*, iv, 163–64), reported that: "a person who is fled thither [i.e. Edinburgh] from England for being author of *Legion's Address* and goes by the borrowed name of Allen (though his true name is Pierce) with some others of his kidney kept the calves head feast at the house of one Fowler in the Cowgate, by which we may see what sort of people they are that libel the present House of Commons". A copy, now in the National Library of Scotland, of *A Dialogue between a Country-Man, and a Landwart School-Master, concerning the Proceedings of the Parliament of England* (Edinburgh, 1705) has a manuscript inscription in an old hand on its title-page: "By Peirce Alias Legion Alias Allen Alias etc." One of the copies of *Legion's Humble Address* in the National Library of Scotland has a contemporary inscription: "This is the address for qch Allan brock newgate prison and ffled to Scotland". In *The Memorial of the Presbyterians* (1706) reference is made to "one P–e, a Broker, (that has kept out of the Way for publishing and dispersing a half Sheet, which was wrote by D.D.F.)". On 30 November 1706 Defoe wrote to Harley that John Pierce, whom he had sent as emissary to the Cameronians, "will merit a pardon for what has past if he performs this service whether he has success or no". In *The Review Review'd: In a Letter to the Prophet Daniel in Scotland*, published probably in April 1707, Defoe was urged to "be civil to poor *Jack Pearse*, who you know was forc'd to travel Northward upon your Account". A letter from Robert Watts to A. Charlett of 6 February 1708, quoted in *Remarks and Collections of Thomas Hearne*, ed. C.E. Doble (1886), ii, 425, says: "The Author of... *The Observator reviv'd* was one *Pearce* an Exchange Broker some time concern'd in ye Paper call'd *Legions Address* & forc'd to fly on that Acct into Holland." Finally, in *An Impartial Survey of Mr De Foe's Singular Modesty and Veracity, in Presuming to Dedicate his Experiment to the Queen* (1710), Defoe was accused of being the author of "*Legion's Address*".

75 The Christianity of the High Church Consider'd

London: Printed in the Year 1704

ATTRIBUTION: Wilson; Trent (*Nation* – as very probably Defoe's), Hutchins, Moore, Novak.

A challenge to the High-Church party, in the person of a Dissenter, published 12 April 1704, i.e. nine days after the Queen, in closing the current session of Parliament, rebuked it for disregarding her exhortations to peace and unity. (On 14 December 1703 the Lords threw out the second Occasional Conformity Bill.) The tract, dedicated to Lord Haversham (who several times spoke against Occasional Conformity Bills), asks the high-flyers how they can possibly justify their aspersions on the Dissenters. Have they not been models of civic propriety ever since the Civil War? If this is not persecution, where is it to be looked for? Are the high-flyers afraid that the financially very prosperous Dissenters might "lessen the

Trade of the Nation"? But this would be absurd, for it would ruin them as well (pp. 14–15). The case for liberty for the Dissenters is not the same as for Papists, since the latter are declared enemies of Protestant institutions.

Benjamin Harris advertised this as "By the Author of *Moderation Maintain'd*", and this latter (Moore, **73**) has a Preface signed "D.F.". However, as explained in our note on **73**, having been arraigned in the *Review* for foisting works on Defoe, Harris removed the offending reference from his advertisements. This therefore seems to cancel the one piece of external evidence for Defoe's authorship.

The internal evidence, though broadly speaking the author shares Defoe's views about the wrongs of the Dissenters, and it would not be absurd to imagine him the author of the work, is not really strong. The reference (pp. 6–7) to the English betrayal of the Protestants of La Rochelle in 1627 clashes slightly with the account given in the *Review* for 8 December 1711, and the allusion to the *Book of Sports* (p. 7) offers no actual verbal parallels with the passages on the same subject in the *Review* for 22 April 1707 and 23 March 1710. The laudatory dedication to Lord Haversham could also be thought a little surprising, since Defoe was soon to come out as a severe critic of Haversham. (This is probably why Lee omitted the work from his list.) One is thus left with no really secure basis for an ascription to Defoe.

84 A True State of the Difference between Sir George Rook, Knt. and William Colpeper, Esq.

London: Printed and Sold by the Booksellers of London and Westminster, 1704

ATTRIBUTION: Wilson (who says, however [i, 281], "It is doubtful whether Mr Colepeper himself was not the author"); Lee, Moore, Novak (as "Probably partly by Defoe").

An account, with a prefatory epistle addressed by William Colepeper to Sir John Holt, the Lord Chief Justice, of the assaults on himself by associates of Sir George Rook, Lord High Admiral – the first of these (by Sir Jacob Banks) taking place in July 1703 at Windsor Castle, where Colepeper was delivering a petition on behalf of the imprisoned Defoe, and a later occurring in the London streets; together with a transcript of proceedings at Colepeper's successful prosecution of Rook's friends Denew, Meriam and Britton before Sir John Holt.

Wilson, and more recently Paula Backscheider in her *Daniel Defoe: His Life* (Baltimore and London, 1989), p. 177 and note, are sceptical about the need to propose Defoe as part author; Trent (*Nation*) says he has "strong reasons" (unspecified) for believing it was written by Colepeper himself; Lee is confident that it was compiled by Defoe, and so is Moore, who even speculates that Defoe was one of the shorthand reporters in court.

Since Colepeper signed the work and there is no *prima facie* reason why he could not have composed it himself, the fact that Defoe might be conceived as having had a hand in it, since he was a friend of Colepeper's and championed him in the *Review*, seems no good reason for assuming that he did.

87 The Protestant Jesuit Unmask'd: In Answer to the Two Parts of *Cassandra*

London: Printed in the Year 1704

ATTRIBUTION: Wilson (as "Most probably" Defoe's); Lee, Trent (*CHEL*), Hutchins, Moore, Novak.

An answer to Charles Leslie's attack on the Dissenters in his *Cassandra* of June 1704. It represents Leslie's attack as a "Jesuitical" disguise for Jacobitism.

Leslie, in his *Rehearsal*, 34 (17–24 March 1705), makes it clear that he supposes Defoe to have been the author. However, one can safely reject this theory, since on pp. 35–36 the author offers a defence of Occasional Conformity, a practice which Defoe never wearied of condemning. It may be added that the tone, both in serious and tediously bantering passages, never suggests him.

92 Persecution Anatomiz'd

London: Printed in the Year 1705

ATTRIBUTION: Lee; Trent (*CHEL*), Hutchins, Moore, Novak.

Written in the person of a Dissenter, a month or so after the failure of the "Tack", it argues that there must have been more behind the attempt to "tack" the Occasional Conformity Bill than mere anxiety for the Church's safety: its secret motive must have been to extirpate the Dissenters altogether and to abolish the Protestant Succession, bringing in French slavery. If such a plan was not *persecution*, where should one look for it? Sacheverell deserves the pillory more than the unfortunate author of *The Shortest Way* (p. 22). It should not be thought, however, that the author condones Occasional Conformity: if the sole purpose of the Bill had been to prevent it, it would have been a good thing for the Dissenters if it had passed.

This tract takes, broadly speaking, the Defoean line on Occasional Conformity, but there are one or two oddities that make the attribution questionable: (1) the eulogy of Lord Haversham in the Dedication of this tract does not seem quite to square with the elaborate attack on him in the *Review* in November of the same year; (2) the name "W–y" is cited several times as that of a furious high-flyer, evidently in mistake for "L[esl]y". This is such a gross error that, even if it were the printer's fault, it would be strange if Defoe overlooked it.

*101 A Letter from Scotland to a Friend in London: Containing a Particular Narrative of the Whole Proceedings against the *Worcester* and her Crew

London: Printed in the Year 1705

ATTRIBUTION: Moore (a tentative attribution only. He says: "I am much less sure of his [Defoe's] authorship than I was in 1939").

A violently chauvinistic attack on the Scots for the execution of Thomas Green, the captain of the *Worcester*. As we argue in *The Canonisation* (p. 104), the discrepancy between this and the cautious and statesmanlike tone Defoe adopted about the *Worcester* affair in the *Review* (26 April 1705) makes it highly unlikely that he wrote it. In a letter to F.H. Ellis, 5 June 1973, Moore says that Defoe certainly knew the tract well, but his present evidence suggests that someone else wrote it.

102 The Ballance: or, A New Test of the High-Fliers of All Sides

London: Printed in the Year 1705

ATTRIBUTION: Trent (*Nation*) (as "Almost certainly" Defoe's); Hutchins, Moore, Novak.

A vigorous attack on the doctrines of passive obedience and non-resistance, arguing that they have no basis in Scripture and are contrary to human reason and experience. Exponents of them should remember that it was the Bishops and lay members of the Church who instigated the Revolution, thereby being as guilty of as absolute a breach of non-resistance "as any

Roundhead or Whig in England". The author says he is no favourer of the
Dissenters' religious opinions, for some of which he has "the last Aversion",
but the way to deal with them is not by persecution. They should be
allowed liberty of conscience, and in return they should renounce all
involvement in political affairs.

The main reason why Trent and Moore ascribed this to Defoe was
because it contains several complimentary references to him. It praises
"Mr. de Foe's *Short Way with the Dissenters*" as an accurate account of the
high-flyers' views (p. 8) and says that his *A New Test of the Church of
England's Loyalty* "was never answer'd" (p. 15) and that the practice of
Occasional Conformity was "not only condemned by the sober Dissenters,
but wrote against by Mr. *de Foe*" (p. 28). It is not clear why this should be
thought to show Defoe's authorship, especially as he is not the only author
complimented by name. Moreover the "Legion Papers" are attacked as
the kind of railing and invective which "is making the Rabble the Judge
and courting Anarchy and Confusion", and the author expresses strong
hostility to the Scottish Presbyterians. The prose style also seems very un-
Defoean.

104 A Collection from Dyer's Letters, concerning the Elections of the Present Parliament

London: Printed and Sold by B. Bragg, 1706 [for 1705]

ATTRIBUTION: Moore.

A selection of extracts from Dyer's *Newsletter*, beginning 3 May 1705,
illustrating Dyer's campaign in favour of the erstwhile "Tackers" in the
election of May-June 1705. An "Advertisement" submits the collection to
"Persons in Authority" as an example of the "mischievous Engines that
have been set at Work for some Years past". (The extracts also give
sympathetic coverage to Drake's High Tory *Memorial of the Church of
England* and its vicissitudes.)

There is a similar though shorter compilation in manuscript in the
Portland Papers (BL, Add. MS. 70022, ff. 182–83), containing some but
not all of the same extracts as well as some others, and Henry Snyder, who
mentions this in his article "Newsletters in England, 1689–1715" in
Newsletters to Newspapers: Eighteenth-Century Journalism, ed. D.H. Bond and
W.R. McLeod (Morgantown, West Virginia, 1977), p. 7, implies that
Defoe was drawing on it in the present tract. However, it is hard to see
anything in the *Collection* or its brief "Advertisement" that would point
specifically to Defoe rather than to any other of Harley's many agents.

108 Declaration Without Doors

[London, 1705]

ATTRIBUTION: Moore; Novak.

A (folio half-sheet) satirical ballad, written as by William Bromley, the high-flying Tory candidate for the Speaker's chair, on the eve of the first meeting of the new Parliament. It makes much play with his youthful travel book *Remarks in the Grande [sic] Tour* (1692), which Harley had recently caused to be republished to embarrass him.

An advertisement in the *Review* for 25 October 1705 reads: " *This Day is Publish'd*; A Declaration without Doors; by the Author of, etc. Sold by the Booksellers of *London* and *Westminster*." (The *Review* for 30 October further advertised, as to be "speedily" published, "An Answer to that Scurrilous and Reflecting Pamphlet, Entituled, *The Declaration Without Doors*".) Wilson, who evidently noticed the earlier advertisement, seems to have assumed, not having seen a copy of the work, that it was a prose pamphlet and described it in his list as a quarto. In this he was followed by Hazlitt, and also by Lee, who (probably on no good evidence) expanded the "etc." to read "of *The True-Born Englishman*". Trent seems to have realised that the prose pamphlet was a ghost, for he omitted the title from his *Cambridge History of Literature* list, though it reappeared in Hutchins's *CBEL* list. The poem is quite effective, but of a kind such as a dozen writers might have turned out. D.F. Foxon, in his "Defoe: A Specimen of a Catalogue of English Verse, 1701–1750", *The Library*, 5th series, 20 (1965), 293, says there is "no clear evidence for Defoe's authorship", and we agree with him.

111 The Case of Protestant Dissenters in Carolina

London: Printed in the Year 1706

ATTRIBUTION: Lee; Trent (*CHEL*), Hutchins, Moore, Novak.

An exceedingly detailed and circumstantial account of the arbitrary proceedings of the "Palatine", Lord Granville, against the Dissenters in Carolina. Lee supposes that, having been briefed by Joseph Boon and ex-Governor Archdale, the representatives of the Carolina Dissenters in London, to write *Party Tyranny: or, An Occasional Bill in Miniature; as now Practiced in Carolina* (Moore, **105**), he obtained "additional information" from them as a basis for the present long tract. The internal evidence for Defoe's authorship of *Party Tyranny* is persuasive; but Lee's account (p. 119) of Defoe's personal dealings with Boon and Archdale appears to be pure speculation (Wilson, who first attributed *Party-Tyranny* to Defoe, makes no mention of them). The same is true of Moore's statement that "Defoe was the acknowledged spokesman for the Carolina Dissenters"; see his article "Defoe's 'Queries upon the Foregoing Act'": A Defense of Liberty in South Carolina" in *Essays in History and Literature Presented by Fellows of The Newberry Library to Stanley Pargellis*, ed. Heinz Bluhm (Chicago, 1965), p. 148. Thus there is no compelling reason for assigning the present tract to Defoe. The intimate knowledge of the domestic history of Carolina shown in it strikes one, moreover, as going far beyond what could be obtained from a mere briefing; nor does the style sound at all Defoean. (It is worth noting that Trent, in his unpublished Bibliography, includes the work mainly out of respect for Lee's intuitions and says that Lee's confidence "may probably suffice to keep that pamphlet under Defoe's name in the bibliographies until a writer with better credentials is pointed at in some contemporary document".)

121 A Letter from Mr. Reason to the High and Mighty Prince the Mob

[Edinburgh, 1706]

ATTRIBUTION: Robert Wodrow; Hutchins, Moore, Novak.

A clever and knowledgeable appeal to the Edinburgh mob not to listen to their would-be advisers Mr. Malice, Mr. Spite, etc., but to one who can show them the great advantages to their trade and manufactures from the proposed Union – these advantages being dependant upon one another like "the links of a Chain".

Moore's note records the existence of three "old manuscript notes" in copies in the National Library of Scotland. Two of these attribute the *Letter* to James (or Captain) Donaldson, while the third – in Wodrow's hand – gives it to Defoe. Donaldson (*fl.* 1713) was an impecunious miscellaneous writer who published several pamphlets on economic affairs (*DNB, q.v.*), and it does not seem impossible that he could have written the *Letter*. At any rate, there are several reasons for doubting Wodrow's attribution to Defoe. Most important is the attitude taken to the Mob here, which contrasts markedly with Defoe's idiosyncratic view – expressed in the *Review* and elsewhere – that in extreme situations the Mob has often been the preserver of liberty. Also worth noting are a number of oddities and Scotticisms in the tract, which seem to suggest a Scottish rather than an English author (e.g. "cognosed", "should to the Kingdom happen", "consumpt", "prohibite").

122 An Answer to My Lord Beilhaven's Speech

[Edinburgh?]: Printed in the Year 1706

ATTRIBUTION: Moore; Novak.

Lord Belhaven (1656–1708) made his famous speech against the Union on 2 November 1706. The present *Answer* goes through the printed version point by point, arguing that, contrary to Belhaven's doom-laden predictions, the Scots have much to gain in the way of trading opportunities and national security by uniting with England.

It is plain from Defoe's letter to Harley of 14 November 1706, and also from his later correspondence with Belhaven himself (see *Review*, 10 July 1708), as well as his poem "The Vision" (1706), that he decided to treat Belhaven's speech as a joke. Thus it seems unlikely he was also the author of this humourless and sanctimonious piece.

126 Considerations in Relation to Trade Considered

[Edinburgh?]: Printed in the Year 1706

ATTRIBUTION: Moore; Novak.

Written in the person of a Scotsman and most probably printed in Edinbugh, this tract is in reply to pamphlets by William Black and others, arguing against these latter that the Scots will not be disadvantaged under the excise and tax arrangements of the Treaty of Union. In the printed catalogue of the Advocates' Library (1873) it is attributed to James Donaldson. Moore notes: "Contains some Scots idioms", interpreting these as a disguise, but fails to mention that, as in **130** and **131** (*qq.v.*), the calculations are worked out in terms of Scottish measures and currency, in a way that it is hard to believe an outsider could have managed. (The contrast with Defoe's *Fourth Essay at Removing National Prejudices*, published almost simultaneously, is glaring.) The tract has a title-page epigraph: "Prov. 18. 17. He that is first in his own Cause seemeth Just; but his Neighbour cometh and Searcheth him." Moore calls this "an obvious and very characteristic allusion to Defoe's own position as an Englishman who wrote as a critical observer in Scotland", but the logic of this is faulty, for there would seem to be no point in Defoe's disguising his hand by "Scots idioms" if his title-page was intended to convey that he was an Englishman. Thirdly, and most importantly, we learn from Defoe's *History of the Union* (p. 94) that it was he himself who settled the vexed question of excise on Scotland's ale and drafted the Amendment to the Treaty dealing with this; yet the pamphlet, though on p. 25 it refers to the crucial Amendment, makes no reference to Defoe. There thus appears to be no good reason to assign this tract to Defoe and strong reason to believe the author to be, as he claims, a Scotsman. See our "Defoe and the 'Tippony Ale'", *Scottish Historical Review*, 72 (1993), 86–89.

127 A Seasonable Warning: or, The Pope and King of France Unmasked

[Edinburgh?]: Printed in the Year 1706

ATTRIBUTION: C.E. Burch, in "Defoe's First *Seasonable Warning* (1706)", *RES*, 21 (1945), 322–26; Moore, Novak.

Despite its lurid title, a sober, low-key statement of the case for the Union. The author, who writes as a Scotsman, warns that rejection of the Union might bring about a disastrous war with England and would certainly deal a fatal blow to the already depressed Scottish economy. Though not an M.P., he has attended some of the debates in Parliament, where he has heard no convincing argument against the Articles.

Burch's case for the attribution rests on correspondences between the political and economic arguments advanced with those found in other Defoe works, and on autobiographical allusions near the end of the pamphlet. "There can be little doubt", writes Burch, "that it is Defoe, proud of his part in the Union proceedings, who is here proclaiming to Englishmen and Scotsmen alike: 'Though I have not the honour to vote in Parliament I have been admitted sometimes into the House'." We can see little or nothing in these correspondences and allusions to connect the tract with Defoe. The work seems very different in style and polemical method from the six *Essays at Removing National Prejudices* which Defoe was publishing at the same period, nor does its theory of parliamentary sovereignty really square with his. Moore (p. 243) offers the information that in his copy there is "a contemporary inscription: 'by Mercenary Dan De ffoe'", but nothing can be built on such an ascription by an unknown hand.

*130 The State of the Excise after the Union

[Edinburgh?]: Printed in the Year 1706

ATTRIBUTION: Robert Wodrow; Trent (Bibliography), Hutchins, Moore, Novak (as "Perhaps by Defoe").

Written partly in answer to William Black's *A Short View of our Present Trade and Taxes* (1706), it offers a brief calculation, conducted in Scottish measures and currency, to show that the rumoured increase of excise liabilities under the Treaty of Union has been greatly exaggerated, and argues that the poor in Scotland will benefit from the new Union arrangements. In the past, since all Scottish ale paid the same duty, brewers tended to brew strong ale, but under the new regulations a "good wholsom" small beer will also become available.

Like **126** and **131**, this shows an extremely intimate knowledge of Scottish habits, and, though published about 1 December, it contains no reference to the Amendment to the Treaty of Union, drafted by Defoe in November, which transformed the whole situation as regards Scottish ale. The idea that this tract is a Scottish impersonation by Defoe does not carry conviction.

Given the date of Wodrow's ascriptions (see Introduction above, pp. xv xvii), they must count as external evidence. However, we are inclined to go along with J.A. Downie in his discussion of another Wodrow attribution to Defoe in "Defoe and *The Advantages of Scotland by an Incorporate Union with England: An Attribution Reviewed*", *PRSA*, 71 (1977), 489–93. Downie here likens Wodrow's methods of reasoning to Moore's. "Defoe wrote tracts in favour of the Union, this pamphlet [*The Advantages of Scotland*] is mentioned favourably in a tract known to be Defoe's, therefore he wrote this one too. Whole groups of pamphlets can be linked together in this way and added to the Defoe canon on no other grounds than that each refers to the others."

*131 The State of the Excise etc. Vindicated

[Edinburgh, 1706?]

ATTRIBUTION: Robert Wodrow; Trent (Bibliography), Hutchins, Moore, Novak (as "Perhaps by Defoe").

A rejoinder to a reply to **130**, *Some Few Remarks upon the State of the Excise after the Union*, by William Black. The author apologises politely for any injury to Black's feelings but proceeds to buttress the arguments of the earlier pamphlet by more detailed calculations – once again largely in Scottish currency and measures. We would apply the same arguments to this attribution as to **130**.

133 The Rabbler Convicted

[Edinburgh, 1706?]

ATTRIBUTION: Robert Wodrow; Trent (*CHEL*), Hutchins, Moore, Novak (as "Almost certainly by Defoe").

A brief and sanctimonious confession, by a Scottish ex-"Rabbler", that reason and conscience have at last convinced him of his folly in joining in riots against the Union and showing "Disobedience to superiour Powers" (elsewhere described as God's "Viceregents here on earth").

Nothing in this tract obviously suggests Defoe, whose known writings in support of the Union appeal to utility rather than to authority. Moore's case for the ascription rests on the "old manuscript note" by Wodrow. Alan Downie's scepticism about Wodrow's attributions (see note on **130**) suggests that it is wisest to follow one's instinct in thinking this unlikely to be by Defoe.

134 The Advantages of Scotland by an Incorporate Union with England

[Edinburgh?]: Printed in the Year 1706

ATTRIBUTION: Robert Wodrow; Hutchins, Moore, Novak (as "Almost certainly by Defoe").

An answer to Patrick Abercromby's *The Advantages of the Act of Security, Compar'd with these of the Intended Union: Founded on the Revolution-Principles Publish'd by Mr. Daniel De Foe* (1706), which had argued that Scotland would benefit more from a union with France than with England. Defoe praised it highly in his *Fifth Essay, At Removing National Prejudices* (1707), p. 8, saying he does not know who the author is, but evidently taking him to be a Scotsman – as did William Black in *A Reply to the Authors of the Advantages of Scotland by an Incorporate Union and of the Fifth Essay, At Removing National Prejudices* (Edinburgh, 1707). J.A. Downie, in the article cited in our note on **130**, sees no reason to suppose that the present tract is by Defoe himself, writing in the guise of a Scotsman, and we agree with him.

135 A Letter concerning Trade from Several Scots-Gentlemen that are Merchants in England

[Edinburgh, 1706?]

ATTRIBUTION: Moore; Novak (as "Probably by Defoe").

A letter from some Scottish merchants in England to their fellows in Scotland, rebutting the arguments of William Black and others against the Union. It rejects Black's plea that the Scottish fish-merchants should be exempted from the Salt Tax, arguing that they actually benefit from it (i.e. from the draw-back when exporting), and it discredits the idea that Scottish beer and ale would carry a disproportionate excise duty. It holds out golden prospects for Scotland from the trade with the American colonies.

The figures given in regard to the Salt Tax (p. 2) and the excise on beer and ale differ from those given by Defoe in his *Fourth Essay, At Removing National Prejudices*. In his *Fifth Essay, At Removing National Prejudices* (p. 26) Defoe remarks that the authors of the present tract give inflated figures for the Scottish West-Indian export trade as it would be under the Union. These discrepancies incline us to regard this attribution as doubtful.

137 A Scots Poem: or, A New-Years Gift, from a Native of the Universe, to his Fellow-Animals in Albania

Edinburgh: Printed Anno Dom., 1707

ATTRIBUTION: C.E. Burch, in "The Authorship of *A Scots Poem* (1707)", *PQ,* 22 (1943), 51–57; Moore, Novak.

A strongly pro-Union poem in heroic couplets, written as by a Scotsman, published just before the final ratification of the Treaty of Union in January 1707. It paints in glowing colours the many advantages Union would bring to his country and answers various objections to the proposed treaty.

Burch's case for the attribution rests entirely on correspondences with other Defoe works. As he says, many of the benefits of Union stressed in the poem – that it would ensure peace, greatly increase opportunities for trade, lead to improvements in fishing, agriculture etc. – are also put forward in works like Defoe's *Essays at Removing National Prejudices*. But as he very fairly admits, "all advocates of Union" used similar arguments. He claims, however, that *A Scots Poem* can be distinguished from other pro-Union propaganda: "Particularly noticeable ... are the author's passionate advocacy of the Union, his extravagant forecasts of the benefits of the Union to Scotland, his garrulousness, his large use of factual details ... his interest in and knowledge of geography, trade and colonisation ... the Puritan ethics of the author". Other distinctive points, according to Burch, are the panegyrics on the Dukes of Hamilton and Argyll and a digression on King William.

It is hard to feel that any one of Burch's points, or all of them together, really clinch the attribution. A broadside reply, *A Short Satyre on the Native of the Universe, The Albanian Animal, Author of The New Years's Gift, or Scots Poem upon the Union*, does not identify the author, though one of four copies in the National Library of Scotland carries a manuscript note: "This seems to be on Defoe." Nothing can be built on such an anonymous note; and there are aspects of the poem which tend to point away from Defoe – for instance the absurdly jingoistic militarism which pictures the Scots planting their banners on the Tiber and the Seine (p. 9); and the eulogies of Argyll and Hamilton, of both of whom Defoe tended to be critical. The sheer *grotesquerie* of the verse style, moreover, places it at a remove from *Caledonia*. F.H. Ellis, in *Poems of Affairs of State*, vii (New Haven and London, 1975), though accepting the attribution, notes how unlike *Caledonia* the poem is and puts down its "lack of energy and high spirits" to physical and emotional exhaustion on Defoe's part. His annotations draw attention to a number of archaic words and spellings and Scottish idioms, which would be very natural if the author were a Scot but less so if Defoe.

Altogether, though one would not absolutely rule out the possibility of Defoe's authorship, there do not seem to be sufficient grounds for even a "probable" attribution.

*143 The Fifteen Comforts of a Scotch-Man. Written by Daniel D'Foe in Scotland

London: Printed in the Year 1706

ATTRIBUTION: Chalmers (as "Supposed to be De Foe's"); Moore.

Moore's note on this piece of doggerel runs: "Attributed to Defoe on the title-page, and from internal evidence probably his, although the title seems quite uncharacteristic of him and the tract itself is inferior in composition to any known to have been written by him." It is difficult to see what "internal evidence" Moore can have been thinking of, beyond the mere fact that the poem is pro-Union. The witless abuse of "Poor lousie, beggar'd *France*, and half starv'd Spain" is in marked contrast with the *Review* for 25 September 1707, where it is admitted that France has in fact had a good year. The spelling "D'Foe" in the title also argues against his authorship.

144 A Discourse upon an Union of the Two Kingdoms

London: Printed for A. Baldwin, 1707

ATTRIBUTION: Moore; Novak (as "Perhaps by Defoe").

A tract arguing the benefits of a Union, largely from an English point of view. It describes it as a choice between a union and a conquest, and says that there is no reason to fear danger for the Church of England, since Presbyterians are not likely to get the better of Anglicans in argument, and the superiority of bishops over presbyters is recognised in the Constitution. Nor, in general, can trade suffer, though a few individual traders may. The author suggests that it might be wise for the Queen to grant a toleration for Scotland, thereby perhaps eventually securing a general conversion to episcopacy.

The approach of this bland and parsonical tract is quite unlike that of Defoe's *Essays at Removing National Prejudices*, and several points in it show the author as (unlike Defoe) very little concerned for Scottish feelings. An implausible attribution.

144a Queries upon the Foregoing Act

[London, 1707?]

ATTRIBUTION: Moore.

The text of the Act to exclude Dissenters from the Carolina Parliament was reprinted as *The Copy of an Act Lately Pass'd in Carolina* and was supplemented by an introductory paragraph and an appendix containing the above-named *Queries*, criticising the Act in much the same spirit as *Party-Tyranny* (1705/6), a work which there is reason to think is by Defoe.

Moore, in "Defoe's 'Queries upon the Foregoing Act': A Defense of Civil Liberty in South Carolina" in *Essays in History and Literature Presented by Fellows of the Newberry Library to Stanley Pargellis*, ed. Heinz Bluhm (Chicago, 1965), 133–55, claims (p. 147) that "The 'Queries' are certainly the work of Defoe; the evidence for his authorship is unusually strong and varied"; but the points he brings forward, such as "the misuse of 'farther' for 'further', as in *The Farther Adventures of Robinson Crusoe*", and Defoe's known "fondness for getting to the heart of an argument by means of a series of inquiries", can hardly be said to carry much weight; and his whole article, as mentioned in our note on **111**, shows a tendency to go beyond the facts. One could well believe these *Queries* to be by Defoe, but the evidence for an attribution hardly seems adequate.

145 Remarks upon the Lord Haversham's Speech

[Edinburgh, 1707?]

ATTRIBUTION: Robert Wodrow; Moore, Novak (as "Probably by Defoe").

An answer, in the person of a Scotsman, to Lord Haversham's speech against the Union delivered on 15 February 1707. It argues, mildly, that Haversham is wrong in supposing anything unusual in independent kingdoms uniting, for history is full of examples, and even offers some instances where the two nations had different religions; also it says that he has not explained his "federal" solution clearly.

There are some queer spellings in the tract, including "Havarsham" in the title, which Moore suspects may have been deliberate "Scotticisms" on Defoe's part.

Defoe has a punchy and ribald attack on Haversham's speech in the *Review* for 22 March 1707, and it is hard to reconcile it with the present bumbling and ineffective tract. One thus would require better evidence before assigning this to Defoe. It may be added that Moore appears to follow Lee in a muddle about another anti-Haversham tract (**149**, *q.v.*), a fact which shakes one's confidence in his opinion about these two tracts.

147 The True-Born Britain. Written by the Author of *The True-Born Englishman*

London: Printed in the Year 1707

ATTRIBUTION: Moore; Novak (as "Perhaps by Defoe").

Despite its title-page, no previous bibliographer accepted this poem as Defoe's. Moore's description of it as presenting "the point of view of an Englishman shortly after the ratification of the Union" hardly prepares one for this ludicrous piece of militaristic triumphalism, which prophesies that the newly-united Britain will "swim to *Lewis* through his Army's Blood". A glance at the *Review* for this period persuades one it is extraordinarily unlikely that Defoe could have written this.

149 A Modest Vindication of the Present Ministry

London: Printed in the Year 1707

ATTRIBUTION: Lee; Trent (*CHEL*), Hutchins, Moore, Novak.

An answer to a speech by Lord Haversham to a Committee of the Whole House on 19 November 1707, in which he attacked the conduct of the war and Prince George's running of the Navy, and also to his earlier speech of 15 February 1707, in which he criticised the Union and made slighting references to the Queen's "She-Favourite" (i.e. the Duchess of Marlborough). It accuses Haversham, with his talk of a "ferment" in the nation, of irresponsible gossip-mongering.

Lee (and it would seem, from his numbering, Moore also) dated the tract to early in 1707, mistaking it for an answer merely to Haversham's speech of 15 February. The tract, very prosy and circumlocutory in style, is markedly different in tone from Defoe's comments on Haversham's later speech in the *Review* (6 and 9 December), in which he treats Haversham entirely as a figure of fun, and this prompts doubt about Lee's attribution.

156 Advice to the Electors of Great Britain: Occasioned by the Intended Invasion from France

[London: J. Morphew, 1708]

ATTRIBUTION: Samuel Halkett and John Laing, *A Dictionary of the Anonymous and Pseudonymous Literature of Great Britain*, 4 vols. (Edinburgh, 1882–88); Trent (*CHEL*), Hutchins, Moore.

An appeal to voters in the coming election to draw the necessary lesson from the recent abortive Jacobite invasion: i.e. that the Tories and so-called "Country Party" are treacherous and unworthy to be put in charge of the destinies of the nation.

It has been demonstrated by Henry L. Snyder, it would seem conclusively, that this pamphlet was written by Arthur Maynwaring and Sarah, Duchess of Marlborough. See his article "Daniel Defoe, the Duchess of Marlborough, and the *Advice to the Electors of Great Britain*", *HLQ*, 29 (1965–66), 53–62, where he reports the discovery of a rough draft of the pamphlet in the Duchess's hand, and a finished draft in Maynwaring's own hand. Alan Downie's discovery of a letter of 5 April 1708 from Maynwaring to the Duchess clinches Maynwaring's authorship even further; see J.A. Downie, "Arthur Maynwaring and the Authorship of the *Advice to the Electors of Great Britain*: Some Additional Evidence",

British Journal for Eighteenth-Century Studies, 2 (1979), 163–66. Moore, in a note added to the second edition of his *Checklist* (p. 244), refers to Snyder's evidence but is not inclined to give up the attribution to Defoe. He admits that the pamphlet "undoubtedly passed through the hands" of Maywaring, and "was apparently edited by him'; but, says Moore, "it has marked characteristics of Defoe's style".

160a A Brief History of the Poor Palatine Refugees

London: Printed and Sold by J. Baker, 1709

ATTRIBUTION: Moore; Novak.

Written in the form of "A Letter to a Friend in the Country", this is an apparently well-informed account of the recent influx of refugees from the Palatinate, the debate about them, and the various charitable measures taken and plans proposed for dealing with them. It gives extensive details of the different towns in Germany from which they have come and enumerates the various places to which it has been proposed to transplant them (e.g. Rio de la Plata, the Canary Islands and the American colonies), arguing (p. 41) that Jamaica – which nobody has yet mentioned – would be far better than all the others. Nevertheless, on the grounds that "people are the riches, honour, and strength of a Nation", it recommends giving them permanent shelter in England and Ireland, and it reports that there is a plan, which "may immediately be put in Execution", for buying a whole manor or parish on their behalf and assigning 100 acres of it to them, at a peppercorn rent, their labourers being immediately put to work in building huts to house them.

The pamphlet presumably belongs to mid August, since it cites the *Gazette* for 6 August (p. 45), and by early September, according to the *Review* (6 and 8 September), the idea of creating a colony for the refugees had been given up and it had been decided to disperse them among different parishes in England.

A comparison with Defoe's own many discussions of the problem in the *Review* (throughout June, July and August), and his later account of an elaborate proposal he claims to have made to Godolphin in 1709 for a colony in the New Forest (see his *Tour Thro' the Whole Island of Great Britain*, ed. G.D.H. Cole, 2 vols. [1927], i, 200–6) suggests that he can scarcely be the author of this tract, despite its similarities to his own point of view and one or two verbal parallels. Of the many points of difference, one may mention that, in contrast to what the present tract says about Jamaica,

Defoe argues in the *Review* that it would be fatal to plant the refugees in an *island* colony. Defoe reports in the *Review* for 2 August that a scheme to buy land for the refugees has been put forward and that he thinks it the best proposal yet, and it would be plausible to connect the present tract with this scheme rather than with Defoe's own.

166 A Reproof to Mr. Clark, and a Brief Vindication of Mr. De Foe

Edinburgh: Printed and Sold by John Moncur, 1710

ATTRIBUTION: Wilson; Lee, Trent (Bibliography), Moore, Novak.

A defence of Defoe, forming part of the paper war begun in 1708 when Defoe, in his as yet unpublished *History of the Union*, accused James Clark, minister of the Town Church, Glasgow, of uttering some inflammatory words in a sermon, which led to a riot. The author writes, he says, in order to put a stop to Clark's "Invective, Unchristian and opprobrious Speeches, against Mr. De Foe, whose Writings make him Famous, since in them is conspicuously to be seen, Eminency of Gifts, Humility of Spirit, Elegancy of Style, Solidity of Matter, Height of Fancy, Depth of Judgement, Clearness of Apprehension, strength of Reason, and ardent Zeal for Truth" etc. The ludicrously eulogistic tone (of which this is only a sample) makes it absurd to imagine Defoe himself as the author. It is worth noting that in his own *Advertisement from Daniel De Foe, To Mr. Clark* (1710?), which is signed "D.F.", Defoe refers to a "Printed Paper" written in his "Vindication" which, although speaking the truth, is too full of "that needless thing called Praise which... the World always calls Flattery... a thing I abhor" (pp. 2–3). J.A. Downie and Pat Rogers, in "Defoe in the Pamphlets: Some Additions and Corrections", *PQ*, 59 (1980), 38–41, describe the *Reproof* as "not necessarily" by Defoe.

168 A Speech Without Doors

London: Printed for A. Baldwin, 1710

ATTRIBUTION: Lee; Trent (*CHEL*), Hutchins, Moore, Novak.

A rejoinder "without doors" to Sacheverell's speech in his own defence at his trial, on 7 March 1710. The tract is an effective Whig polemic, drawing solid reasons from law and history for regarding Sacheverell's "No resistance" doctrines as absurd, and rising at moments to satirical eloquence (e.g. p. 17). Nothing in Lee's account (p. 165), however, indicates why he attributed it to Defoe. Trent, in his Bibliography, confessed that he had "been able to discover no clinching argument in favour of Defoe's authorship" and admitted that his own acceptance was based on a "general feeling", on Lee's authoritativeness, and on "the fact that I can pick out no other writer whose authorship of the excellent pamphlet seems more plausible".

169 The Age of Wonders

[London]: Printed in the Year 1710

ATTRIBUTION: Moore; Novak (as "Attributed by J.R. Moore, but doubtful").

A hard-hitting ballad, evidently written in the summer of the election year 1710, lampooning the high-flying madness which has led the nation to want to get rid of a nobly patriotic Treasurer (Godolphin) and Parliament in favour of covert Jacobites, and to denigrate the Marlboroughs after all the Duke has done for his country. The plan, once this has been achieved, is to wipe out Government borrowings by a "sponge" and either carry on the war at the expense of the nation's creditors or fudge up a shameful peace on France and the Pretender's terms.

F.H. Ellis, in *Poems of Affairs of State*, vii (New Haven and London, 1975), p. 462, assumes somewhat arbitrarily that this is the "most impudent Ballad" that Defoe mentions in a letter to Harley of 5 September 1710, and he finds several suggestive parallels with other writings certainly and probably by Defoe, noting particularly that Defoe twice quotes an isolated couplet from it in the *Review*. But the poem, and especially its last stanza, is so personally insulting to Harley that it hardly seems safe to ascribe it to Defoe, who had recently re-entered Harley's service. Frances Harris has in fact found proof in the Blenheim MSS that it was one of a number of short pieces printed and distributed at the expense of Harley's political adversary the Earl of Sunderland; see *Factotum* no. 9 (August 1980), 12–13.

172 Instructions from Rome, in Favour of the Pretender

London: Printed and Sold by J. Baker [1710]

ATTRIBUTION: Wilson (as "Perhaps, his [Defoe's] production"); Lee, Trent (*CHEL*), Hutchins, Moore, Novak.

A knockabout anti-Sacheverell satire, in the form of instructions from the Pope, dictated by his grand patron Lucifer, to his "dear children" the Jacobites as to how best to undermine the Protestant establishment.

The grotesque, "colourful", neo-Elizabethan style of this burlesque may be illustrated by the following extract:

> Think not to put off all your *Ware* at once; down right Popery at first dash is frightful; But those that Keck at it whole, will swallow it handsomely minc'd. First, Tinge People with a preparative Blew, and then Sause 'em with the Colour of *Scarlet Whore*; begin with our most plausible Principles. The Vulgar never mind the Tail of the Business, yet there lies the Stings. When the Needle's once through the Thred will follow; some serious Truths must be deliver'd, the better under those Palliations to disseminate our profitable Errours, so a Stink offends more when Concomitant with some weak Perfume, which it hath *Pro vehiculo* than when 'tis single. (p. 8)

The style is not uncommon in journalism of Defoe's period but is not met with in any of his own known writings. Thus it seems rash to attribute this tract to him without some external evidence. Though it may be conceded that, other things being equal, one could imagine him as the author of this ironical reference to himself:

> Endeavour to suppress that Damn'd *Review*, that's a plaguey Fellow; Nothing but a miracle wrought by a Power not related to us, has preserv'd that Wretch to be a Scourge to our Faction. A second *Observator*; a second *Tutchin*, whom we cowardly Murder'd for exposing our slavish Doctrines.

Wilson's ascription (iii, 112) is typically casual – "The following, advertised in the *Review* for the 11th of May, was, perhaps, his production" – and it could well be that later bibliographers gave it more weight than it laid claim to.

174 The Recorder of B[anbu]ry's Speech to Dr. Sacheverell

London: Printed in the Year 1710.

ATTRIBUTION: Moore; Novak (as "Attributed by J.R. Moore").

An imaginary speech of welcome to Sacheverell on his arrival in Banbury, during his "progress" through the west country, saying that, if even an ape received a civic welcome here (as happened in Queen Elizabeth's day), how much more is a reception due to a "Person of so much greater Merit". The Recorder hopes Sacheverell will press with "still more Assurance" for a new election, so that "Ale may again run down our Streets like a Stream".

No internal evidence appears to point directly to Defoe. This is the first of a series of skits upon Sacheverell's "progress" through the west country after his trial, attributed by Moore to Defoe: i.e. numbers **174, 175, 180, 181**. Of these, much of **175** and the whole of **180** were reprinted in **181**. Moore claims that **181** is "closely analogous to passages in the *Review* for 13 and 27 July 1710", and it is fair to assume that this is his reason for assigning the whole group to Defoe; however, the claim does not stand up to scrutiny (see our comment on **181**), and accordingly the whole chain of attributions has to be regarded as suspect. (The ascription of these tracts to Defoe in W.A. Speck's edition of F.F. Madan's *Critical Bibliography of Dr. Henry Sacheverell* [Lawrence, Kansas, 1978] is presumably based on Moore's *Checklist*.)

175 The Banb[ur]y Apes

London: Printed and are to be sold by R. Mawson [1710]

ATTRIBUTION: Moore; Novak.

A facetious chapbook style burlesque of Sacheverell's reception by the mayor and corporation of Banbury on 2 June 1710, during his "progress" through the west country after his trial. The Banbury dignitaries are depicted as monkeys, in reverse allusion to the occasion when a mayor and corporation did homage to Queen Elizabeth's ape. This tract is incorporated in the longer *A New Map of the Laborious and Painful Travels of our Blessed High Church Apostle* (**181**, *q.v.*).

177 The Modern Addresses Vindicated, and the Rights of the Addressers Asserted, by D. De Foe

London: Printed for J. Morphew, 1710

ATTRIBUTION: Moore.

Some extracts (slightly adapted) from Defoe's *The Original Power of the Collective Body of the People of England* (1702), misapplied (see p. 7) so as to appear an encouragement to Queen Anne to dismiss the Godolphin ministry and dissolve Parliament.

It is not clear exactly in what spirit this crude piece of trickery was perpetrated, but it is impossible to suppose Defoe himself responsible; hence it cannot be regarded as a separate item in his bibliography.

180 Dr. Sacheverell's Disappointment at Worcester: Being a True Account of his Cold Reception There. In a Letter from a Gentleman in that City to his Friend in London

London: Printed and Sold by J. Baker. 1710.

ATTRIBUTION: Moore; Novak (as "Attributed by J.R. Moore").

An account, in the form of a letter dated "Worcester, July the 18th 1710", of Sacheverell's arrival in Worcester during his "progress" through the west country and of how the Bishop of Worcester succeeded in ruining his triumph by forbidding citizens to go to meet him and church bells to be rung and by having a mob-leader, together with the musicians in Sacheverell's cortege, arrested.

Moore comments that this is a "jesting abridgement of a genuine communication dated 15 July which was advertised in the *Post-Man* (25 July): *The Worcester Triumph … Being Part of a Letter from a Gentleman in Worcester to a Friend in London*". This is somewhat misleading, since (1) *The Worcester Triumph* is itself mildly "jesting" in tone. (2) It is not, in its details (e.g. the numbers of Sacheverell's attendants etc.) very close to the present tract. (3) The present "Letter" is dated 18 (not 15) July. (4) *The Worcester Triumph*, though longer, claims to be only "part" of a *Letter from a Gentleman in Worcester to a Friend in London*. Boyer reprinted *The Worcester Triumph* in his *History of the Reign of Queen Anne, Year the Ninth* (1711), pp. 205–6, where he describes it as a "Genuine Letter", which is no doubt why Moore refers to it as a "genuine communication"; but Madan also records a tract entitled *Dr. Sacheverell's Progress from London … In a Letter from a Gentleman … to his Friend in London*, a fact which indicates that the "Letter to a Friend in London" idea was being widely used.

181 A New Map of the Laborious and Painful Travels of our Blessed High Church Apostle

[London]: Printed in the Year 1710

ATTRIBUTION: Moore; Novak (as "Probably by Defoe").

A fanciful-facetious account of Sacheverell's "progress" through the west country. It incorporates *The Ban[bur]y Apes* (**175**) and *Dr. Sacheverell's Disappointment at Worcester* (**180**).

   Moore describes it as "closely analogous to passages in the *Review* for 13 and 27 July 1710", but this can hardly be said to be the case, for, apart from the difference in style, they contradict each other on matters of fact. The present tract describes Sacheverell's reception at Bridgnorth as triumphal, a vast mob of 3,500 horse and 3,000 foot-pads attending, whereas the *Review* (27 July) says he was "hiss'd and forsaken" there.

*182 High-Church Miracles

London: Printed and Sold by A. Baldwin, 1710

ATTRIBUTION: Moore (as "Very probably, not certainly, Defoe's"); Novak (as "Perhaps by Defoe").

A poem in heroic couplets satirising the inconsistencies of the high-flying party, with explanatory notes.

   Moore gives no reason for attributing this to Defoe, and F.H. Ellis, who goes along with the attribution in his edition of *Poems on Affairs of State*, vii (New Haven and London, 1975), p. 442, makes, it must be said, a very weak case for it, suggesting, for example, that the phrase about "washing the *Aethiop* white" (l. 26) came into Defoe's head because he was involved, just then, in a controversy about the coal trade.

183 A Short Historical Account of the Contrivances and Conspiracies of the Men of Dr. Sacheverell's Principles

London: Printed and are to be Sold by A. Baldwin, 1710

ATTRIBUTION: Moore; Novak (as "Probably by Defoe").

A brief and pedestrian account of three plots against the Protestant interest in England by men of "Sacheverell's principles": (1) The Popish Plot; (2) The "sham Whig" plot (i.e. Rye House Plot); (3) The French-aided plot of the summer of 1690, when a French invasion fleet came near to destroying the English Navy. It quotes from the seditious Jacobite "liturgy" circulated in 1690.

It is not clear why this colourless piece, which in style does not seem at all to suggest Defoe, was attributed to him by Moore.

184 Four Letters to a Friend in North Britain: Upon the Publishing the Tryal of Dr. Sacheverell

London: Printed in the Year 1710

ATTRIBUTION: Moore.

Written in response to the Sacheverellite cry of "the Church in danger", it gives a brief history of the activities of the high-flyers from the beginning of the reign, accuses the High-Church party of appealing to non-resistance doctrines as a cloak for plans to regain power by restoring the Pretender, and rebukes the House of Lords for passing such a light sentence on Sacheverell.

This was attributed to Arthur Maynwaring by John Oldmixon in his *Life and Works of Arthur Maynwaring* (1715), p. 102, and to Robert Walpole by his son Horace in *A Catalogue of the Royal and Noble Authors of England, Scotland and Ireland* (1806), iv, 218. Henry Snyder supports the Maynwaring ascription convincingly in "Daniel Defoe, Arthur Maynwaring, Robert Walpole, and Abel Boyer: Some Considerations of Authorship", *HLQ*, 33 (1970), 133–53, pointing out the existence of an early draft of the pamphlet in Maynwaring's hand. See also Pat Rogers, "The Authorship of *Four Letters to a Friend in North Britain* and Other Pamphlets Attributed to Robert Walpole", *Bulletin of the Institute of Historical Research*, 44 (1971), 229–38.

185 Seldom Comes a Better

London: Printed in the Year 1710

ATTRIBUTION: Moore; Novak (as "Perhaps by Defoe").

Tells how "a certain *Great Man*" (i.e. Louis XIV) makes himself a nuisance to all the neighbouring estates, including that of "*a very Good and Wise Lady*" (i.e. Queen Anne), till at last she brings a suit in Chancery against him, on behalf of her neighbours, being helped in this by a wise Chief Counsellor and a prudent Chief Steward. Unfortunately she listens a little too much to the woman who dresses her (i.e. Abigail Masham), who herself is under the influence of "a *Kinsman*, a cunning Fellow, a Pettifogger, and of a very ill character, that never was true to any Cause he ingag'd in" (i.e. Harley), and she unwisely dismisses a faithful old servant.

Pat Rogers, in "Addenda and Corrigenda: Moore's *Checklist* of Defoe", *PBSA*, 75 (1981), 60–64, calls this attribution "dubious", and doubt is also cast on it by A.W. Bower and R.A. Erickson in their edition of Arbuthnot's *The History of John Bull* (1976). They say (p. xx) that it is "highly improbable" that in 1710 Defoe would have described Harley, his employer, in this way. We would endorse this.

186 A Letter from a Dissenter in the City

London: Printed for A. Baldwin, 1710

ATTRIBUTION: Moore; Novak (as "Attributed by J.R. Moore but doubtful").

An emollient plea from a Dissenter, who signs himself "Irenaeus Americus", to his co-religionists, to be peaceable in regard to the recent changeover to a Tory administration. The author declares that he does not know Harley but claims to have often "waited on" St. John upon "Affairs of Importance" and says that Envy itself cannot deny that he is a wise man.

It is hard to see any good reason for ascribing this to Defoe, and we are happy to go along with Novak's verdict in the *NCBEL*.

189 A Letter from a Gentleman at the Court of St. Germains ... Translated from the French Copy, Printed at Cologne by Peter Marteau

London: Printed in the Year 1710

ATTRIBUTION: Moore; Novak (as "Perhaps Defoe, but also ascribed to Maynwaring").

An effective anti-Jacobite satire, in the form of a letter from an Irishman at the court of the Pretender to a friend in England, explaining the right strategy for promoting the Pretender's cause. It is no use, it says, to think of imposing him by force: the proper way is by quietly fomenting faction – especially between the Dissenters and their low-Church allies, thus putting both at the mercy of the furious high-flyers. In this, their great stand-by will be the *clergy*, who are venal and worldly, and whose Church occupies an absurdly illogical position. (Who are they to condemn schism, being themselves schismatic?) The publisher explains how an officer friend of his in the Allied army found the letter by accident after the siege of Douai. He is publishing it, he says, out of affection for Great Britain and for the Protestant cause. The tract was cited with enthusiasm in the *Review* for 31 October 1710, and several times later, having already been discussed approvingly in the *Observator* for 6–9 September.

John Oldmixon, in his *Life and Works of Arthur Maynwaring* (1715), p. 324, claims that Maynwaring wrote this, or that a friend of his did so with his assistance. However, Pierre des Maizeaux (1673–1745), a refugee French philosopher and journalist, also claims to have written it, in various draft petitions and letters now in the British Library (Add. MS. 4289); and the fact that "Pierre du Marteau of Cologne" was a favourite fictitious imprint used by Franco-Dutch publishers for "dangerous" publications would help to support the claim of Des Maizeaux, who was in constant touch with Dutch editors and publishers: see L. Janmart de Brouillant, *La liberté de la presse en France* (Paris, 1888). There are, however, certain puzzles which complicate the issue. At all events, it can be demonstrated from one or two translator's slips that the French version is the original; and, given the wildly inaccurate nature of Defoe's French, this seems to rule him out as author. See further our article, "Daniel Defoe and *A Letter from a Gentleman at the Court of St. Germains* (1710)", forthcoming in *Etudes Anglaises*.

190 A Condoling Letter to the Tattler

London: Printed and Sold by S. Popping [1710]

ATTRIBUTION: Moore; Novak.

A "letter" telling Isaac Bickerstaff, the author of the *Tatler* [i.e. Steele], who has recently been a prisoner in a spunging-house, that he should pay attention to this lesson from Providence – those who pass judgment on their fellow humans' faults have a particular obligation not to commit the same ones themselves. Mr. Bickerstaff has been witty lately about "State-Barometers" and "Church-Thermometers", so why did he not mention a certain "Oeconomical Barometer, or Family Weather-Glass"? The author has been told that the author of the *Review* brought one of these down from the Moon and makes some mention of it in *The Consolidator* (p. 18) – though he cannot vouch for this. It is, at all events, a useful engine (though the author of the *Review* does not seem to have made much use of it himself), and he will describe it. It is marked off in degrees running from Madness, through Extravagance, to Plenty and the middle degree, FAMILY, and on to Parsimony, Covetousness and Madness again. Bickerstaff should learn from it the reproaches due to a man who, "having a plentiful Revenue, and no Family-Charge, profusely wasts it in Extravagances and Excess".

One is inclined to reject the attribution to Defoe since in the *Review* for 14 December 1710 he writes of Steele (who devoted no. 229 of the *Tatler* to those who had "*annotated, retattled, examined,* and *condoled*" him) that "I have always thought that the weakest step the *Tatler* ever took ... was to stoop to take the least Notice of all the Barkings of the little Animals that have *Condol'd* him, *Examin'd* him ... He should have let Envy bark, and Fools rail". It is worth adding that Defoe's references to Steele at this time tend to be very flattering, though his tone changed a year or two later.

One does not find a reference to an "Oeconomical Barometer, or Family Weather-Glass" on p. 18 of the *Consolidator*. Thus the author seems to be representing it as the kind of thing that the author of the *Consolidator* brought down from the Moon, which indeed it is. One guesses that it was because of this reference to the *Consolidator* that Moore attributed the tract to Defoe.

194 A Supplement to the *Faults on Both Sides*

London: Printed for J. Baker, 1710

ATTRIBUTION: Trent (*Nation*); Hutchins, Moore, Novak.

This was a contribution to the pamphlet war sparked off by Benjamin Hoadly's *Thoughts of an Honest Tory*, an attack on the Tories published on 26 June 1710, less than a fortnight after the dismissal of Sunderland which marked the beginning of the replacement of Godolphin's Whig administration with a new Tory ministry under Harley. Among the answers to Hoadly was *Faults on Both Sides* by Simon Clement, and *Sir Thomas Double at Court*, by Charles Davenant. *A Supplement*, which appeared towards the end of October, is particularly concerned to defend the Whigs against Davenant's attacks on them.

It takes the form of a dialogue between two displaced politicians: Steady, a convinced Whig, and Turn-Round, formerly a Whig, who became a Tory but is now returning to the Whig fold. Turn-Round retains a good opinion of Harley and is inclined to hope for the best for the nation, but he is rebuked by Steady, who rehearses recent political history from the

Revolution onwards to show what a damaging role the Tories have always played, whether in office or in opposition. Granting the truth of this, Turn-Round wonders whether it will be the same now, since, as Defoe has been arguing in the *Review*, "The New Ministry... Whatever they are in Opinion... must be Whiggs in Practice". Steady, however, fears that bringing so many Tories into the government will lead to "a mad High Tory Administration" (p. 53). He foresees the ruin of credit and a capitulation to France on terms less advantageous than those held out for by the Godolphin ministry.

It is evident from the account in his Bibliography that Trent was persuaded to attribute *A Supplement* to Defoe because of the presence of a number of references to works by him, in addition to the citations from the *Review* already mentioned. These certainly are prominent (see for example pp. 31, 37, 44, 53, 64), but they tend to spell out Defoe's full name in a way which would be very natural in another writer but much less so if he were referring to himself. Moore, as well as noting an allusion to *A Letter from a Gentleman at the Court of St. Germains* (an ascription we consider extremely doubtful; see our note on **189** above), suggests that there is "a characteristic bantering allusion" to Defoe's *Essay upon Loans*, but in fact the passage he quotes is obviously a swipe at Davenant's *Sir Thomas Double at Court*, which opens with two characters discussing their antecedents.

What neither Trent nor Moore mentions is that the pamphlet seems designed to fuel doubts and fears about the new Tory administration and is personally distinctly hostile to Harley. Since Defoe was by this time once more in Harley's pay and was arguing in the *Review*, at the same moment, that Whigs had nothing to fear from the new administration, the probabilities are against his being the author.

198 R[ogue]'s on Both Sides... By the Same Author

London: Printed for John Baker, 1711 [for 1710]

ATTRIBUTION: Trent (*CHEL*); Hutchins, Moore, Novak.

Published actually December 1710, this was a savage attack on the late Godolphin administration – its corruption, determination to prolong the war, deification of its leaders, bullying of the Queen, etc. – in the form of definitions of "Old Whigs", "Modern Whigs", "Old Tories" and "Modern Tories". The "Modern Tories" are credited with the public-spirited virtues of the "Old Whigs" of Revolution stamp, and the "Modern Whigs" are branded with the worst vices of the "Old" (high-flying) Tories. The title alludes to Simon Clements's *Faults on Both Sides* of October 1710 (another piece of Harleyite propaganda), and so, presumably, does "By the Same Author".

Defoe's authorship is made most improbable by the passage on p. 16 about hypocritical "Modern Whigs", who "sacrifice those very liberties they pretend to be zealous for ... Thus they attacqu'd the very being of the House of Commons, not only by their *Black Lists*, *Legion Letters* and *Kentish Petitions*, but by writing against the very constitution of the House of Commons".

199 A Short Narrative of the Life and Actions of his Grace John, D[uke] of Marlborough ... By an Old Officer in the Army

London: Printed for John Baker, 1711

ATTRIBUTION: Moore; Novak.

A eulogistic defence of Marlborough, by an "Old Officer" who had served with him in King William's wars, against the various rumours and scandals about him disseminated in the *Examiner* and elsewhere – for instance that he betrayed Dunkirk to the enemy. The tract is full of campaign details, as if by a participant, and there are circumstantial accounts of the author's encounters with Marlborough and the Duchess.

Moore, in his *Daniel Defoe: Citizen of the Modern World* (Chicago and London, 1958), pp. 255–256, suggests various reasons why Defoe might have wished to adopt the disguise of "An Old Officer in the Army" in order to produce this eulogistic defence of Marlborough, at a time when several members of the Harley administration were planning to impeach him: it would prevent detection by Harley, it would justify his revealing "Within doors" (inside) knowledge, it would give him "a literary freedom which he needed in his finest writing", etc. He gives no external evidence for the attribution and, in its absence, we find little force in his hypotheses. See our *Canonisation*, pp. 119–120, for a fuller discussion. It may be added that on 10 January 1712 Defoe wrote to Harley in terms extremely hostile to Marlborough ('God ... has Moved you No doubt to Take This Most Necessary step of Deposeing The Idol Man, who Coveted to Set himself up as The head of a Party", etc.).

199a Vox Dei et Naturae: Shewing the Unreasonableness and Folly of Imprisoning the Body for Debt

London: Printed in the Year 1711

ATTRIBUTION: Moore.

A fervent plea against surprise arrest and imprisonment for debt, arguing that it is against the injunctions of Scripture and contrary to the practice of most humane nations, ancient and modern.

In our article "Defoe and Imprisonment for Debt: Some Attributions Reviewed", *RES*, n.s., 37 (1986), 495–502, we argue, on the strength of Defoe's discussions of imprisonment for debt in the *Review*, that, whilst he condemned many abuses in the current treatment of debtors, he regarded imprisonment for debt itself as essential to England's commercial prosperity. On this basis we would reject the present tract and also a later expansion of it, *The Unreasonableness and Ill Consequences of Imprisoning the Body for Debt* (1729) (**506**, *q.v.*).

200a The Quaker's Sermon: or, A Holding-Forth concerning Barabbas

London: Sold by A. Baldwin, 1711

ATTRIBUTION: Moore.

A "Quaker" sermon, likening the treatment of Sacheverell to that of Barabbas and comparing the treatment of Marlborough by the Tories to Hannibal's betrayal by Hanno.

Moore explains his reasons for this late attribution in "Defoe's Persona as Author: The Quaker's Sermon", *Studies in English Literature*, 11 (1971), 507–16, saying that the arguments used in defence of Marlborough are "virtually the same which Defoe had used as far back as 1706 in *Remarks on the Letter to the Author of the State-Memorial* and very recently in *Seldom Comes a Better* (1710), *Atalantis Major* (1711), and especially *A Short Narrative of the Life and Actions of His Grace John, D. of Marlborough* (1711)". In fact, Defoe in a letter to Harley of 10 January 1712 showed himself extremely hostile to Marlborough (see note on **199** above), and *Seldom Comes a Better* (**185**) and *A Short Narrative* (**199**), *qq.v.*, seem unlikely to be by Defoe. (On p. 516 of his article Moore mistakenly supposes that the "modern name" which is meant to be suggested by "Hanno" is "Henry St. John", whereas it is evidently "Hanmer" – Sir Thomas Hanmer having chaired the committee which reported adversely on Marlborough.)

211 The Scotch Medal Decipher'd

London: Printed for S. Popping, 1711

ATTRIBUTION: Moore; Novak (as "Probably by Defoe").

An attack on the Edinburgh Faculty of Advocates for accepting a silver medal, depicting the Pretender and bearing an inscription prophesying his return to the throne, from the Duchess of Gordon. The tract demonstrates, by citing statutes, that this was an act of high treason, deserving heavy penalties, and says that it is high time that English high-flyers disassociated themselves from their Scottish fellows.

This humourless tract takes quite a different line from the ironical one adopted by the *Review*, which said that the more Scotch medals the better, for the Jacobites had an infallible knack of putting themselves in the wrong. (See *Review* for 4 August 1711.) No obvious reason suggests itself why Moore should have attributed this to Defoe.

212 A Speech for Mr. D[unda]sse Younger of Arnistown

London: Printed for J. Baker, 1711

ATTRIBUTION: Samuel Halkett and John Laing, *A Dictionary of the Anonymous and Pseudonymous Literature of Great Britain*, 4 vols. (Edinburgh, 1882–88); Trent (*Nation*), Hutchins, Moore, Novak.

Published on 30 August 1711, this is an imaginary speech by James Dundas the Younger, in pseudo-Scottish spelling, defending himself from the charge of having urged the Edinburgh Faculty of Advocates to accept a medal in honour of the Pretender, presented by the Duchess of Gordon. Who can believe, says Dundas, that the Advocates should have accepted the medal on 30 June and gone back on the decision a fortnight later? It is more likely that Ridpath's *Flying-Post*, which made this report, was lying. But, he continues, even if, for argument's sake, it were agreed that he made a speech in favour of accepting the medal, was he not merely acting according to the sentiments of the Addresses made to Queen Anne the previous year? It was these very Addresses which had persuaded him that "the right of the Crown is Hereditary and Indefeasible, and mon always deshend to the fuist Prince of the Bluid" (p. 12). It seems hard that he should be punished when the authors of these Addresses have not been condemned.

This is quite a clever tract, and it is certainly not impossible to think of Defoe as the author. He had written frequently about the high-flying

Addresses in the *Review* and reported on the "Scotch Medal" affair in the issues for 31 July and 4 August. He wrote to Harley about it on 27 August, pointing out the dangers and suggesting that he be sent to Scotland again. Furthermore, a friend of his wrote to him on 15 August, encouraging him to "keep up the alarm about the *Medal*" and suggesting that Dundas's activities might "affoord you some work of your happy pen".

None of this is quite sufficient to clinch the attribution, however, and the absence of other proved examples of Defoe using mock-Scottish spelling at length is a further reason for caution. Until some further evidence is forthcoming it seems that this attribution must be regarded as no more than possible.

213 A True Account of the Design and Advantages of the South-Sea Trade

London: Printed and Sold by J. Morphew, 1711

ATTRIBUTION: Trent (*Nation*); Hutchins, Moore, Novak.

A tract written on behalf of Harley's South Sea Company, which has recently begun trading. It takes a view not unlike Defoe's in *An Essay on the South-Sea Trade* (1711), in the *Review*, and in his letter to Harley of 17 July 1711: that, whereas it is absurd to think the Spanish will ever allow a general free trade in South America, they might well accommodate themselves to the existence of a British settlement there and turn a blind eye to their colonists' trading with it. On the the other hand, in contrast to the drift of Defoe's known writings on this subject, where the emphasis is all on peaceful colonisation (see, e.g., the *Review* for 17 July 1711), this tract envisages military action against the French in South America. It insists that the French have exploited the war to gain control of South America and its trade, settling garrisons all over Peru and Chile, so that, if Britain is to make a settlement in the region, it will have to dislodge the French by force of arms. (One of the advantages of the South Sea scheme will be the support it can lend to this.) The tract goes on to picture the South Sea Company co-operating with the Madagascar pirates, who are active in the South Seas.

Abel Boyer praises the tract, saying it was written by "a particular friend" of his (*Political State*, September 1711, 527), a description he is hardly likely to have applied to Defoe. This, and the discrepancy of outlook mentioned above, put this attribution in a certain amount of doubt.

217 Reasons why a Party among us ... are Obstinately Bent against a Treaty of Peace with the French ... By the Author of the *Reasons for Putting an End to this Expensive War*

[London]: Printed for John Baker, 1711

ATTRIBUTION: Lee; Trent (*CHEL*), Moore, Novak.

Argues that the Whigs' objections to the peace negotiations are motivated by party-political ends, just like their attacks on Harley's South Sea scheme. They have run down credit for totally unpatriotic reasons and have confused "the poor Common People". Near the end, it turns to "a late Pamphlet, which calls it self *An Answer*, to our former *Reasons for Putting an End to this Expensive War*", and offers a defence of (as it repeatedly calls him) "the Author of the *Reasons*" against this *Answer* (which was actually entitled *A Letter to a High-Churchman, in Answer to a Pamphlet Intitled, Reasons Why this Nation*, etc. (1711).

  Despite the claim made on the title-page, it is very hard to believe that this is by the same author as *Reasons Why this Nation*, since it is written in a grotesquely stilted style, full of strange inversions of syntax and "eth" endings, and is altogether unlike the earlier pamphlet. One is led to suppose that either the author, or Baker, or both linked it to the other, very successful, pamphlet to boost sales. Equally, it is almost impossible to picture Defoe writing such an incompetent piece. Trent was driven to suppose that he was trying to disguise himself, but he offers no explanation as to why he should have wanted to.

218 Armageddon: or, The Necessity of Carrying on the War

London: Printed for J. Baker [1711]

ATTRIBUTION: Crossley; Lee, Trent (*Nation*), Moore, Novak.

Written in the person of a moderate Whig, this argues that the Whigs as a body, as opposed to a few trouble-makers, harbour no belief that the Tory administration is conducting nefarious and secret negotiations for a separate peace. Whigs and Tories want the same thing, peace with honour, and merely differ about the best way to attain it: the Whigs hold that there might be profit in one more campaign. The clamour about clandestine negotiations raised by Abel Roper in the *Post-Boy* and others is probably actually a High-Church stratagem to embroil Britain with her allies.

On pp. 23–24 it describes the argument in favour of a partition of the Spanish monarchy as a "Cavil", easily confuted; and, since Defoe was tireless in advocating a partition (see, e.g., the *Review* for 16 June and 13 October 1711), this can be regarded as a clinching reason for rejecting the attribution. The work was, however, advertised in the *Review* for 13 November 1711.

Trent records an old manuscript note attributing the tract to Asgill.

219 The Ballance of Europe

[London]: Printed for J. Baker, 1711

ATTRIBUTION: Lee; Trent (*Nation*), Moore, Novak.

A consideration of the new international situation caused by the succession of the Archduke Charles to the Imperial throne. It deprecates factiousness on both sides in Britain and reviews the various schools of opinion about the possibility of a peace and about what should be done with the Spanish monarchy – should it go to the Emperor, or to Philip V, or should there be a partition? The idea of a partition is referred to as an "old and Exploded notion"; the dangers of "exorbitancy" if the monarchy went to the Emperor are painted in dark colours; and the author comes down in favour of allowing the whole Spanish dominions to remain with Philip V, on condition he enters into a firm alliance with the Confederates and restrictions are placed on France's trade with Spain.

Defoe was so insistent, after Charles became Emperor, that the only acceptable basis for a peace was a partition (see our note on the previous entry) that we can safely reject this attribution. It should be noted, though, that an advertisement in the *Post-Man* for 30 October-1 November 1711 describes *The Ballance of Europe* and the third edition of *Reasons Why this Nation Ought to Put a Speedy End to this Expensive War* (Moore, **216**) as "Both by the Same Author". The author of a pamphlet, *A Caveat to the Treaters* (1711), which discusses *The Ballance of Europe* together with two pamphlets known to be by Defoe, notes that on p. 26 it warns of the supreme menace of French arms, and he writes: "Nothing can more plainly demonstrate the Inconsistency of this Writer, if it be Mr. *Foe*, than to compare this *Review* of Sept. 1 with what he has writ since." This, if anything, could be said very slightly to support our own view.

220 Worcestershire-Queries about Peace

London: Printed for S. Popping, 1711

ATTRIBUTION: Moore; Novak (as "Attributed by J.R. Moore, but little internal evidence").

Tom Flockmaker, a clothier from Worcester, meets the narrator in London and complains that he hardly recognises his old Whig coffee-house acquaintances. He expected some sympathy from them in the present depressed condition of the clothing trade, for they used to be men who understood trade, but now they only seem interested in war and conquest. They overhear him and reply that they are all for peace, but for a *good* peace, whereas there is a "parcel of Fellows... that are for giving away *Spain*, the Centre and the Staple of our Commodities" (p. 6). He thereupon puts a series of "Queries" to them, one of which is, could not Spain be left in the possession of Philip V, so long as he and his grandfather Louis XIV are bound by strict commercial treaties to safeguard British interests?

   It could be argued that, given that this is written in the person of a rustic clothier who might be supposed not much interested in the balance of Europe, it is not incompatible with Defoe's views as put forward in the *Review*. (The issue for 13 October 1711 certainly lays much stress on the need for a commercial treaty as a part of any general treaty.) However, this is hardly in itself an argument for his authorship, and we are inclined to go along with Novak's verdict in *NCBEL*.

   The phrase "Worcestershire Queries" echoes a pamphlet – not otherwise connected, so far as one can see – by Harley and Davenant, entitled *A Letter from the Grecian Coffee-House: In Answer to the Taunton-Dean Letter. To which is Added, A Paper of Queries Sent from Worcester* (1701). See J.A. Downie, "Robert Harley, Charles Davenant and the Authorship of the *Worcester Queries*", *Literature and History*, 3 (1976), 83–99.

225 A Defence of the Allies and the Late Ministry

London: Printed and Sold by J. Baker, 1712

ATTRIBUTION: Crossley; Trent (*Nation*), Hutchins, Moore, Novak.

A point-by-point answer to Swift's *The Conduct of the Allies*, arguing not against peace negotiations as such, but against any abject surrender to the French, and defending the Dutch as valuable allies to whom Britain owes much gratitude.

In our "Defoe and the Dutch Alliance: Some Attributions Examined", *British Journal for Eighteenth-Century Studies*, 9 (1986), 169–82, we argue that it is not inconceivable that this competent but stylistically lifeless pamphlet could be by Defoe, but that the case for his authorship is not really strong. A further small point against Defoe is that this author is dismissive of the suggestion that the war should be carried to the West Indies (pp. 24–27), whereas Defoe was a great supporter of this strategy, which he thought would cut off the sources of French and Spanish wealth. (See *Review*, 18 and 20 January, 1711.)

226 A Justification of the Dutch

London: Printed for J. Baker, 1712

ATTRIBUTION: Moore; Novak.

An attack on Swift's *The Conduct of the Allies*, as Jacobite propaganda, representing the Dutch as disinterested throughout and arguing that the Emperor cannot be blamed for dragging his heels in the peace negotiations, since it is his indisputable right to be given the Spanish dominions.

This bland and unconvincing tract puts forward a scheme so contrary to the view hammered at by Defoe in the *Review* from October 1711 to the summer of 1712, i.e. that the only solution to the Spanish problem is a partition, that one can confidently reject it. See our article cited in the previous entry. Paula Backscheider, who, in her *Daniel Defoe: His Life* (Baltimore and London, 1989), p. 582, disagrees with our verdict on the attribution, as put forward in our article, oddly makes no reference to the above point, which is central to our argument. A further piece of evidence is that this tract reproduces *A Letter from Monsieur Pett[ecum] to Monsieur B[u]ys* (1710), a strong attack on Harley and the Tories to which it would be hard to imagine Defoe wishing to give currency at this time.

227 No Queen: or, No General

London: Printed and Sold by the Booksellers of London and Westminster, 1712

ATTRIBUTION: Trent (*Nation*); Hutchins, Moore, Novak.

A vicious ironical attack on Marlborough, recently dismissed by the Queen, in the guise of an implausible defence: he could not have been guilty of the avarice, disloyalty and low political manoeuvres of which he has been accused, since no one could possibly be so ungrateful to a bountiful patroness such as Queen Anne, etc. (No such excuse can be offered for the party which – perhaps against his will – made use of him.)

The passage on pp. 19–21 attacking "the Observators, Reviews, and the Pamphleteers of that Time" for having attempted to have Marlborough impeached in 1709, as a way of overthrowing the Godolphin ministry, seems most unlikely to be by Defoe: why should he want to blacken the reputation of the *Review*? The actual tone about Marlborough in the *Review* is quite different.

Acording to Trent's Bibliography this was attributed by the Revd. William Stoughton, in his *Secret History of the Late Ministry* (1715), p. 219, to "a certain sort of a North Country Pedler in High-Church Politicks", an "Artick Politician".

229 Peace, or Poverty

London: Printed and Sold by John Morphew, 1712

ATTRIBUTION: Crossley; Trent (*Nation*), Hutchins, Moore, Novak (as "Probably by Defoe").

An unremarkable piece, arguing that the Allied war aims have now been achieved, at much cost to Britain, and there seems no good objection to concluding a peace – though there is no intention of making a separate one. The Dutch, it is true, are against a peace; but why should the British go on fighting a war simply to profit them? There are those who say that Britain should invade France and dethrone Louis XIV; but it is not at all certain that she could, and if she were to regain her former dominions in France it is doubtful whether it would benefit the ordinary English person.

The tract, though published on 27 January 1712, seems to reflect the situation of some weeks earlier. (It does not mention the opening of the Utrecht peace conference.) It has no very close echoes of Defoe's numerous writings about a peace in the *Review* at this period, though it is broadly speaking on the same side, and one can see no obvious reason for believing it to be his.

229a Some Queries Humbly Propos'd upon the Bill for a Toleration to the Episcopal Clergy in Scotland

[London, 1712]

ATTRIBUTION: Moore.

A half-sheet attacking the Scottish Toleration Bill introduced in the Commons in January 1712 and passed in March. As Moore points out in "Defoe Acquisitions at the Huntington Library", *HLQ,* 28 (1964), 45–57, the line of argument is close to Defoe's in letters to Harley at the time and in several issues of the *Review* (e.g. 29 January 1712). However, Robert Wodrow, writing on 2 February 1712, specifically says that "The querys anent the Episcopall Bill are drawn up at London by Sir Peter King, Sergant Sprat, Mr. Carstairs, and others"; see his *Analecta*, 3 vols. (Edinburgh, 1842–43), ii, 7.

229b A Letter from a Gentleman in Scotland to his Friend at London

London: Printed in the Year 1712

ATTRIBUTION: Moore.

A letter, dated 29 January 1712, from an English gentleman in Scotland to a highly-placed friend in England, complaining that the Bill now pending in Parliament for a toleration of the use of the liturgy by Episcopal Dissenters in Scotland is a clear breach of the Union treaty, liable to enflame the Presbyterians, most of whom did not want the Union in the first place, and a potential danger to the future safety even of the Church of England.

The author's views are broadly in line with those of Defoe, who criticised the Bill vehemently to Harley (24 January 1712) and in the *Review* for 29 January and 2 and 5 February 1712. But it is hard to find any very close parallels of thought and phrasing with those known Defoe items, so this seems to be only a "possible" attribution, rather than a "probable" one.

232 The History of the Jacobite Clubs

London: Printed for J. Baker, 1712

ATTRIBUTION: Crossley; Trent (*Nation*; but not in *CHEL*), Moore, Novak (as "Perhaps by Defoe").

An account of the Jacobite clubs, founded in competition with the Calf's Head clubs, and especially of one frequented by Abel Roper and Dean Swift, and of the celebration they planned for the supposed day of the proclamation of peace, 25 September 1712 (one of Roper's miscalculations). The final pages modulate from facetiousness into a more earnest attempt – though on the part of a writer "inclinable to favour the Whigg Interest" – to discredit the notion that the Harley ministry was planning a Jacobite *coup*.

There seems no obvious reason to connect this tract with Defoe, and it would have been a dangerous one for him to write at this period of close intimacy between Harley and Swift. The noisily facetious style of the earlier pages also does not suggest him.

Trent, in the *Nation*, called it "a by no means unlikely but, for certain reasons, a doubtful ascription" and subsequently dropped it.

*235 Plain English

London: Printed and Sold by J. Woodward, 1712

ATTRIBUTION: Trent (*Nation*; tentatively only); Hutchins, Moore, Novak (as "Perhaps by Defoe").

A blustering and feebly-argued diatribe, aimed at "some Men (who need not be nam'd)", against current Whig anti-Government propaganda, representing it as springing from mere envy and lust for power. (It refers to the anti-Jacobite procession planned to coincide with Marlborough's arrival at Greenwich on 17 November 1711, but suppressed by Government action.)

It is hard to see any good reason for attributing to Defoe a piece so unlike him in style and approach.

239 The Present Negotiations of Peace Vindicated

London: Printed and Sold by the Booksellers, 1712

ATTRIBUTION: Trent (*CHEL*); Hutchins, Moore, Novak (as "Almost certainly by Defoe").

A euphoric tract, published in June 1712, arguing that Britain is in a very prosperous condition, so that Whig suspicions of the present and past peace-negotiations are mean-minded and ill-founded. They would only be justified if it could be proved that Britain and the Allies were planning a partition of the Spanish dominions, instead of giving them all to their rightful possessor, the Emperor – and this is an absurd idea.

One may feel confident that this is not by Defoe, considering his repeated advocacy, after the election of Charles III as Emperor in October 1711, of a partition of the Spanish dominions as the only rational basis for a peace-settlement. See our note on **218** and the *Review* for 17 July 1712.

The tract, which gives a most implausible defence of the Tory ministry, then suffering much odium over the secret "restraining orders" given to the British troops, could just conceivably be a Whig "banter" on the Tories.

243 The Justice and Necessity of a War with Holland

London: Printed and Sold by the Booksellers of London and Westminster, 1712

ATTRIBUTION: Trent (*Nation*); Hutchins, Moore, Novak.

Published on 26 July 1712, it argues that the balance of power in Europe must be maintained and exorbitant power at all costs reduced. Accordingly, if the Dutch, disregarding the Queen's urgent pleas for peace, were to abet the Emperor in pursuing the war, with the whole Spanish monarchy as the ultimate prize, it would be the duty of Britain, which holds the balance of Europe in its hands, to declare war on them – for all that "War with *Holland* is a Thing of that Consequence that every true Protestant of this Nation should deprecate with the greatest Fervency and Zeal imaginable".

As we argue in our article "Defoe and the Dutch Alliance" (see note on **225**, above), this could be said to be broadly in agreement with the views expounded in the *Review*, though Defoe often gave warning there, in even more vehement, indeed apocalyptic, tones, that war with the Dutch was always fatal to Britain. However, the prose style, with its long winding "periodic" sentences, stuffed with legal phraseology ("whereof", "the said ", "albeit" etc.), suggests the laboured prose of a lawyer rather than that of a practising journalist and is almost impossible to associate with Defoe.

244 An Enquiry into the Real Interest of Princes in the Persons of their Ambassadors

London: Printed and Sold by J. Baker, 1712

ATTRIBUTION: Lee; Trent (*CHEL*), Hutchins, Moore, Novak.

A discussion of the recent diplomatic quarrel at Utrecht, when the servants of the French envoy, Mesnager, made faces at those of the Dutch envoy, the Count de Rechteren, and the Count encouraged his own servants to take revenge. The author carefully examines the issues involved and concludes that the Dutch envoy was in the wrong, and that the Dutch should have hastened to make amends, as Queen Anne did when the Russian ambassador was arrested for debt. However, he does not think it reflects well on either of the principals: they should not have allowed a trifling business like this to interrupt such important proceedings.

A competently-written and well-mannered piece – unlikely, one feels, to be by Defoe, who, in the *Review* for 1 April 1712, attacked such diplomatic fooleries with an altogether more unbridled scorn.

246 Hannibal at the Gates: or, The Progress of Jacobitism

London: Printed for J. Baker, 1712

ATTRIBUTION: Chalmers (as "Supposed"); Wilson (as "Doubtful"), Lee, Trent (*CHEL*, but not in his Bibliography), Hutchins, Moore, Novak.

Published about 30 December 1712, it gives a history of the extraordinary persistence of the Jacobite threat, fomented by the high-flyers and proving even fiercer after the Act of Settlement of 1701. It describes how the Jacobites have aspersed the House of Hanover and have held out delusive hopes of the Pretender's converting to Protestantism, and it draws attention to ominous signs during recent weeks, when gentlemen celebrating King William's birthday in Gracechurch Street were attacked by a High-Church mob and treated by the Tory City authorities as malefactors. (The pamphlet was re-issued by Baker in 1714 with fourteen additional pages at the beginning, replying to a tract entitled *Hannibal Not at Our Gates*.)

The purpose of this violently Whiggish tract becomes clear in its final pages, where it sarcastically gives thanks for the present "Pure, Orthodox, and True *Church of England* Administration" and cites the opinions of the latter's spokesman, the author of the *Review* ('an Authority not to be question'd", as it ironically calls him), giving Defoe's views a Jacobite twist (p. 39). These concluding pages show plainly that the tract cannot be by Defoe himself.

247 A Strict Enquiry into the Circumstances of a Late Duel

London: Printed for J. Baker, 1713

ATTRIBUTION: Lowndes' *Bibliographer's Manual* (1858); Lee, Trent (*CHEL*), Hutchins, Moore, Novak.

An attack on the rumours spread in the Tory press (cf. Swift's *Journal to Stella*, 15 November 1712) that the duel (on 15 November) in which the Duke of Hamilton and Lord Mohun killed each other had been deliberately engineered by the Whigs, using Mohun's second, General MacCartney, as their agent, and that MacCartney had stabbed Hamilton as he lay on the ground. The tract argues that the challenge must have come, not from Mohun as alleged, but from Hamilton himself, and that the quarrel was a purely private one.

Lee (i, 222) cites the pamphlet as a disinterested intervention by Defoe: "Ill as the Whigs had used Defoe, he could not suffer the party to be falsely branded with this horrid deed." However, Defoe's letters to Harley at this time, in which his language against the Whigs is very violent, make such a venture *prima facie* rather improbable; and since nothing in the style seems to suggest him, this must be regarded as an implausible attribution.

249 Not[tingh]am Politicks Examin'd

London: Printed for J. Baker, 1713

ATTRIBUTION: Crossley (as "Not improbably Defoe's"); Trent (*Nation*), Hutchins, Moore, Novak (as "Probably by Defoe").

Published on 21 February, a Whiggish attack on the recent *Observations upon the State of the Nation*, assuming it to be by the Earl of Nottingham and pointing out its various inconsistencies, false prophecies and ill-concealed signs of personal resentment.

The bombastic rhetoric and long winding "Ciceronian" sentences of this tract are so utterly unlike Defoe's ferocious ironies towards his old enemy in the *Review* for 21 and (especially) 24 February as to remove all likelihood that he was the author. (Moore attempts to explain the stylistic anomaly by saying the tract was "apparently written in great haste and in anger"; Trent adopts the "disguise" theory.)

254 An Account of the Abolishing of Duels in France

London: Printed for John Morphew, 1713

ATTRIBUTION: Moore; Novak.

A documentary history of the attempts to suppress duelling in France, with the full text, in translation, of the edict against duelling by Louis XIV of 1679. The Preface says that the tract is intended for the improvement of the British people, who also suffer from this scourge, and that it is rendered seasonable by some strictures on the subject made from the throne.

The translation of the 1679 edict had already appeared as a Supplement to vol. 1 of the *Review* in 1705. However, this is hardly proof that the translator was Defoe or that he was the author of the Preface and the other translations in the present volume (especially since the Preface seems, if a little ambiguously, to imply that the tract is the work of more than one hand.)

259 The Trade of Scotland with France Consider'd

Edinburgh: Printed by James Watson, 1713

ATTRIBUTION: Moore.

Two letters from a Scotsman, originally published in *Mercator*, nos. 19 and 20 (4 and 9 July 1713), giving detailed reasons why the Treaty of Commerce with France, defeated in the House of Commons the previous month, would have benefited Scotland.

A letter from the Scottish M.P. Sir Alexander Cumming (*c.* 1670–1725) to Harley, dated 21 December 1713 (BL Add. MS. 70221), reveals him as the author of these letters. "As for the Commerce bill which I was so much blamed about, as being the author of all those Mercators said to be writ from Scotland, and the procurer of the Letters signed by the Merchants there, approving of our conduct in relatione to that Bill, tho it was not fitt for me to Own those facts, yet I ventured to assert that those who afterward opposed the Commerce Bill would be Lookt upon as Enemys to Scotland. "

261 The Honour and Prerogative of the Queen's Majesty Vindicated

London: Printed for John Morphew, 1713

ATTRIBUTION: Moore; Novak (as "Probably by Defoe").

Written in the person of a country Whig, this addresses Richard Steele as a fellow-Whig, saying that his *Guardian* of 7 August, which asserts that England "EXPECTS" the demolition of Dunkirk, has alienated all those who, like the author, have hitherto enjoyed his charming essays: for it takes an intolerably dictatorial tone towards the Queen. Furthermore, it contradicts what another Whig writer, George Ridpath, has been saying in the *Flying Post*, i.e. that Dunkirk is of no importance. Steele is doing the Whig cause no good by letting the Tories see how divided they are.

As the linking of Steele with Ridpath suggests, the pamphlet is a Tory satire. It was in fact attributed by Boyer (*Political State*, vi, 188) to Mrs. Manley, along with *Reasons concerning the Immediate Demolishing of Dunkirk* (1713), on the basis of contemporary rumour; and although Moore says this attribution is mistaken, he offers no evidence for Defoe's authorship.

We know, of course, that Defoe was very hostile to Steele (see his letters to Harley of 19 February and *c.* 10 March 1714). It is also noteworthy that both pamphlets were advertised (sometimes along with *Memoirs of Count Tariff*) in *Mercator* during August and September. In the absence of any compelling internal evidence, however, this does not seem enough to warrant an attribution to Defoe.

265 A Letter from a Member of the House of Commons... Relating to the Bill of Commerce

London: Printed and Sold by J. Baker, 1713

ATTRIBUTION: Trent (*Nation*; a tentative attribution only); Hutchins, Moore, Novak (as "Probably by Defoe").

The author, who writes as a Tory and Churchman, explains to his friend in the country how Parliament came to make the amazing mistake of rejecting the Bill of Commerce – of which he supplies the text. The truth is, he says, that two lords (Anglesey and Abingdon) managed to persuade

the "men in power", quite falsely, that the whole Church party was
opposed to the Bill. The arguments brought against the Bill at the Bar of
the House by spokesmen for various commercial interests were very easy to
refute, and the Dutch would be the real gainers from continued trade
barriers against France.

The author of a retort to this tract, *Remarks on a Scandalous Libel, Entitul'd*
"A Letter from a Member of Parliament, etc.", in which the ... Falsities and
Absurdities of the Mercator are Expos'd (1713) – it has been attributed to
Oldmixon – says there are "but two Wretches upon Earth that could write
so villainous a Libel", and he makes it fairly plain that he means William
Pittis and Defoe. The reference to "Mercator" in his title is thus not a
direct attribution to Defoe but merely a reference to the well-known
Mercator standpoint. The tract itself, published about 30 June, is broadly
speaking on the same side as *Mercator* but uses somewhat different – that is
to say, unrelated – arguments.

According to Boyer's *Political State*, Baker was arrested for printing the
tract but was released upon declaring the identity of the author, who was
a Tory. Nonetheless, says Boyer, the *Post Boy*, and Boyer himself, suspect
that the author is really a Whig in disguise. The abusive treatment of the
Lords Anglesey and Abingdon shows, as Boyer implies, that the author has
no compunction in exposing the internal divisions of the Tory party – at a
time when, one has the impression, Defoe was giving whole-hearted
support to the beleaguered Tories.

Altogether, though one would not rule out Defoe's authorship, the basis
for an ascription to him does not seem very solid.

266 Whigs Turn'd Tories

London: Printed for J. Baker, 1713

ATTRIBUTION: Chalmers (as "Supposed"); Lee, Wilson, Trent, Hutchins, Moore,
Novak.

Argues, in the person of a Churchman, that the disputes between Whigs
and "Hanover Tories" etc. are really only about the application of words
– like "Faction", "Schism", "Tory", "Whig". The true enemy is the
Jacobite Papist, and the criminal doctrines of the Roman church have
been exposed by (among other historians) Bishop Barlow. If Papists are to
be given toleration, they ought to be made to wear a distinctive dress and
make a declaration of their papistical beliefs (about the right of the Pope
to dethrone monarchs and of Catholics to murder heretics) before a
magistrate.

A terribly laborious and foolish piece, stuffed with interminable quotations and paraphrases of Bishop Barlow and altogether very unrealistic and inept. Wilson describes it as "Another work assigned to De Foe", evidently alluding to Chalmers's doubtful attribution, and Lee appears to have passed on the attribution without actually seeing a copy, for he gives no pagination. A wholly implausible ascription.

270 Proposals for Imploying the Poor

London: Printed for J. Baker, 1713

ATTRIBUTION: Crossley; Trent (*Nation*), Hutchins, Moore, Novak.

A proposal for remedying the public "grievance" of street-begging by founding a "College of Industry" on the banks of the Thames, where the able poor could be employed in handicrafts (spinning, leather-work etc.), but especially in fishing (thereby fulfilling a need, for fishery has been neglected in the county of Middlesex). The Queen would bestow wealthy preferments at her disposal upon clergymen ready to organise this charitable work and willing for a portion of their stipend to go towards it. Various officers would need to be appointed and boats provided. There would have to be a regular inspection by the Lord Mayor and Aldermen, on which occasion they would be given a fish dinner. Prisoners for debt could be allowed to join the college, and inmates would be encouraged to emigrate to the plantations.

This exceedingly sketchy and unpromising scheme is unlikely to have come from Defoe, the author of *Giving Alms No Charity* (1704), a work which condemns all such work-houses as quite the wrong answer to mendicancy, there being no shortage of work in England.

272 Memoirs of John, Duke of Melfort

London: Printed for J. Moor, 1714

ATTRIBUTION: Hutchins; Moore, Novak.

Published 6 February 1714, a brilliant fictitious "Memoirs" of the Pretender's adviser in France, John Drummond, first Earl and titular Duke of Melfort (1649–1714), who died in January 1714. This Whiggish tract employs the device of entering sympathetically into the thought-processes of an enemy, showing up the folly and deviousness of the Pretender by viewing him through the eyes of a loyal but clear-headed supporter. It lends credibility to certain myths, such as that the Sacheverell affair was concocted in the court of the Pretender; and it has Melfort foresee events which did in fact take place, for instance the French delays in demolishing Dunkirk. Melfort's parting advice to his master is that the right time to stage a Jacobite rising would be when the new Parliament assembles – that is to say in February 1714, when this pamphlet was published. Part of the purpose of the tract is to represent Argyll as the Pretender's most dangerous enemy – a sound prophecy, for he played a decisive role in securing the Hanover succession at the Queen's death.

We know of no solid evidence to connect this tract with Defoe, though it must be said that its depiction of Harley as a man of mystery and a "perfect Labyrinth", whose motives the Pretender can never fathom, is very reminisicent of the later picture of him in Defoe's *White Staff* pamphlets. However, the pamphlet, which is very hostile to the Tory administration and goes out of its way to paint the late Godolphin ministry in rosy colours, would come strangely from Defoe in February 1714 when, the evidence is, he was giving the beleaguered Harley loyal support. Moreover, in letters to Harley and in *Atalantis Major*, Defoe revealed himself as very critical of Argyll.

All in all, though one could well imagine Defoe writing this effective and ingenious work, there do not seem adequate grounds for assigning it to him.

276 A Letter to Mr. Steele

London: Printed for J. Baker, 1714

ATTRIBUTION: Crossley; Trent (*Nation*), Hutchins, Moore, Novak (as "Probably by Defoe").

A response to Steele's *Letter to a Member of Parliament concerning the Bill for Preventing the Growth of Schism* of 3 June 1714, saying that, despite a prejudice against the Whiggish Steele, as is natural in a Tory and a member of the Church of England, the author has read Steele's attack on the Schism Bill and is with him in opposing it. (1) Because it shows ingratitude towards the Dissenters, considering the role they played in resisting James II. (2) Because it might ruin the English wool trade, which is largely in the hands of the Dissenters. (3) Because it will injure the Church of England, exposing it to the wiles of Jesuits, who are eager to drive a wedge between British Protestants. It argues that the right of Dissenters to run their own schools and academies must have been "implied" in the Toleration Act, and eminent Dissenting divines, like Bates, Owen, Howe, Mead and Baxter, must have felt easy on this score.

This is an effectively-written pamphlet, in a style one could well imagine to be Defoe's, but (despite Crossley's confident ascription) nothing in it specifically points to Defoe, and one or two things argue slightly against the attribution. For instance, in other writings, e.g. *The Weakest Go to the Wall* (1714), pp. 20–21, and a letter to Harley of 21 May 1714, Defoe blames the Dissenters for their negligence in not stipulating for the right to run their own schools and academies at the time of the Toleration Act. (In his *Letter to the Dissenters* of 1713 Defoe also warned them that their schools and seminaries were, strictly speaking, illegal.) Further, the tract's tone towards Steele contrasts sharply with Defoe's very harsh one in letters to Harley at this period.

277 The Remedy Worse than the Disease: or, Reasons against Passing the Bill for Preventing the Growth of Schism

London: Printed for J. Baker, 1714

ATTRIBUTION: Wilson; Lee, Trent (*CHEL*), Hutchins, Moore, Novak.

Published in early June, this is an attack on the Schism Bill, then pending, in the form of an address to a "Noble Earl" whom the author got to know in the last year of William III's reign. It recalls the peace and neighbourly behaviour in England which instantly followed the Toleration Act of 1689 and reflects on the absurd consequences that would follow from the present Schism Bill: it would even prevent Dissenters from attempting to convert the heathen. On pp. 15–16 there is a long quotation from Milton's *Areopagitica*. A few pages later the author reprints a pamphlet entitled *A Brief Discourse of Toleration and Persecution, etc.* which, he says, he wrote on "a particular Occasion" but thinks will be found relevant to current events. It argues that magistrates can and should have no jurisdiction over private beliefs, only over outward acts, and describes persecution as always the worst of evils. (Protestants have, in the past, been as arrant persecutors as High Churchmen and Papists.)

Wilson gives no reason for assigning this to Defoe, though he praises its sentiments highly; and none of the bibliographers appears to have taken a view as to when, or whether, *A Brief Discourse* was separately written or published, or whether the "Noble Earl" was any particular individual. The orotund style does not immediately suggest Defoe, nor do the tract's learned classical allusions, and the business about *A Brief Discourse* would need some explaining before one could safely attribute this to Defoe.

283 A Secret History of One Year

London: Sold by A. Dodd, 1714

ATTRIBUTION: Boyer; Lee, Trent (*CHEL*), Hutchins, Moore, Novak.

The tract, published in November 1714, argues that people are afraid that George I may make the same mistake as William III in not dealing severely enough with those who betrayed their country during the preceding reign. The author shares this view but wishes it to be explained that the accusation against William of having proceeded to employ the very men who had been accomplices of James II's tyranny is in fact unjust. Initially, he gave office to those who had been active supporters of the Revolution, and it was only when these disappointed him, proving avaricious and corrupt, that he began to employ one-time courtiers of James. In this connection he relates an account given him by a "venerable Gentleman" (an erstwhile M.P. and member of Council) of the conversation which this Gentleman had with a certain "noble Lord", at a meeting of William's supporters during the troubled early days of 1701, and how he reminded the Lord of the true, if "secret", history of the first year of William's reign.

The tract was ascribed to Robert Walpole by Walter Scott, in vol. 13 of his edition of the *Somers Tracts*. Moore dismisses Scott's attribution as "erroneous".

This absurdly repetitive and incompetent piece of writing can, one feels, hardly be by Defoe: the bumbling dialogue between the "venerable Gentleman" and the "noble Lord" almost reads like parody.

284 Tories and Tory Principles Ruinous

London: Printed for J. Baker, 1714

ATTRIBUTION: Trent (Bibliography); Moore, Novak (as "Probably by Defoe").

A disquisition on English history, from Charles I onwards, purporting to show that the Tories have always been disastrous bunglers, bringing disaster on themselves and on all whom they were involved with. Discusses the late Harley administration as a signal example of this theory. Says that the defence of Harley in the *White Staff* tracts is quite unconvincing. Ends with an excerpt from *Atalantis Major*, adapted as a satire on the Tories.

Trent, who included the tract in his Bibliography, took the quotation from *Atalantis Major* (1711) (Moore, **196**) as a clinching argument for Defoe's authorship; but, evidently, there would be nothing to stop another author from using and adapting that witty piece. The denigration of the *White Staff* pamphlets and their defence of Harley would seem to be a much stronger argument against the attribution.

285 Impeachment, or No Impeachment

London: Printed for J. More, 1714

ATTRIBUTION: Boyer; Trent (*Nation*), Hutchins, Moore, Novak (as "Probably by Defoe").

Argues that if the erstwhile Tory leaders Harley, Bolingbroke and Harcourt are to suffer for their part in the "monstrous and villainous" (p. 15) management of the peace negotiations, then their accomplices like the Duke of Shrewsbury, the Earl of Anglesey and the Bishop of Bristol ought to suffer equally – whereas they are now basking in court favour.

We have argued in "The Lost Property Office: Some Defoe Attributions Reconsidered", *PBSA*, 86 (1992), 245–67, that to accept all twenty-four of the items concerned with the fall of Harley which Moore attributes to Defoe, a series alternating (sometimes within a matter of a week or two) between savage attacks and ingenious defences, is more or less impossible, at all events without vastly more in the way of external evidence. In our view, the weight of evidence, as well as simple human probabilities, are against Defoe having published violent attacks on Harley and his administration at this time or, as in the previous pamphlet, repudiating his own defences of him.

In regard to the present tract it would also seem unlikely that Defoe (though admittedly a reckless man) would have been so abusive of the Earl of Anglesey ("the warmest Votary of the Goddess *Persecution*") and of his Jacobite activities in Ireland, at a moment when he was awaiting trial for an earlier offence against Anglesey (i.e. his hand in an attack on Anglesey in the *Flying Post*).

*286 The Bristol Riot ... By a Gentleman who Attended the Commission

London: Printed for J. Roberts, 1714

ATTRIBUTION: Moore (as "Very probably, not quite certainly, Defoe's"); Novak (as "Perhaps by Defoe").

Published on 4 December, an account of the riot in Bristol on the occasion of the King's coronation and of the beginning of the trial, as by one of the special commission sent to investigate it.

Now thought to be by John Oldmixon: see Pat Rogers, "Daniel Defoe, John Oldmixon and the Bristol Riot of 1714", *Transactions of the Bristol and Gloucestershire Archaeological Society*, 92 (1973), 145–56.

287 The Pernicious Consequences of the Clergy's Intermedling with Affairs of State

London: Printed for J. Baker [1714?]

ATTRIBUTION: Moore; Novak (as "Perhaps by Defoe").

An attack on the age-old habit of the clergy of interfering in political affairs, in defiance of the teachings of Christ and the Apostles. Who else but the clergy, it asks, led Charles I to destruction? The need for a law to restrain them is plain to all rational men. (The King's "Injunctions" to the clergy "not to intermeddle in affairs of state" were published on 20 December 1714.)

Though this anticlerical diatribe is aimed at the high-flying clergy and Sacheverellites, its windy and furious rhetoric never for a moment suggest Defoe.

Misere Cleri (1718) (**394**, *q.v.*) is merely a re-issue of this with very minor amendments.

*288 A Full and Impartial Account of the Late Disorders in Bristol

London: Printed for J. Roberts, 1714

ATTRIBUTION: Moore (as "Certainly by the author of *The Bristol Riot*, who was very probably Defoe"); Novak (as "Perhaps by Defoe").

A sequel to **286** (*q.v.*), containing further details of the riot and an account of the trial, now completed.

Now thought to be by John Oldmixon. See **286**.

290 Strike While the Iron's Hot

London: Printed and Sold by S. Keimer, 1715 [for 1714]

ATTRIBUTION: Crossley; Trent (*Nation*), Hutchins, Moore, Novak.

A bellicose Whiggish tract, published actually in December 1714, saying that these early days of King George's reign are the time to break the power of "prime ministers" and seditious clergy. The King should make it a criminal offence to preach or write that "the Church is in danger", and the present ministry should seize the chance to show they are not imitating the personal greed of their predecessors – otherwise it will be in vain for them to criticise such "infamous" schemes as that of William Paterson for a financial "spunge".

The hostility to the "evil" ministry of Harley and to "prime ministers" in general do not suggest Defoe, nor does the unrealism of its anticlerical poposals. Further, his *Essay upon Public Credit* was attacked in 1714, in a tract attributed to Toland, as a covert argument for a "spunge". The style, which runs to well-organised "periodic" sentences, also does not sound like him. (The unrealism and violent anti-clericalism make one wonder whether the tract might not be by Toland.)

291 Memoirs of the Conduct of Her Late Majesty and her Last Ministry ... By the Right Honourable the Countess of ―――

London: Printed and Sold by S. Keimer, 1715

ATTRIBUTION: Crossley; Trent (*Nation*), Hutchins, Moore, Novak.

The tract attempts to exculpate the Harley ministry from the charge of making a dishonourable peace, on the grounds that the whole initiative for a peace came directly from the Queen, who took a leading part in the negotiations, and that Harley and his ministers were careful to obtain ratification from Parliament for every step they took.

The anonymous pamphlet *Queen Anne Vindicated from the Base Aspersions of Some Late Pamphlets* (1715) (sometimes ascribed to William Pittis) asserts (pp. 5–6) that the present pamphlet and *The Secret History of the Secret History of the White Staff* (1715) are by the same hand, that of the author of *The Shortest Way with the Dissenters*. As this indicates, the present pamphlet belongs to the (bibliographically speaking) extremely complicated story of the *White Staff* pamphlets, written in defence of Harley in 1714/15 – i.e. *The Secret History of the White Staff*, parts 1–3, and *The Secret History of the Secret History of the White Staff*, and the many rejoinders to these, both Whig and High Tory. We are of the opinion that Defoe wrote all three parts of *The Secret History of the White Staff* and, despite the puzzles that this involves, that he also wrote *The Secret History of the Secret History*, but that he is not the author of the present tract. Our argument rests on literary grounds. It is very hard to believe that the author of such ingenious and subtle productions as the *White Staff* pamphlets, which manage to present so cunning and plausible a defence of Harley – one based on his known weaknesses of character – could contemporaneously be producing such a clumsy and hopelessly implausible polemic as *Memoirs of the Conduct of Her Late Majesty* (of which Trent writes, "I am afraid that the Countess was a fraud who could not have deceived a baby"). See further our article cited in note to **285** above.

292 Treason Detected: In an Answer to ... *English Advice to the Freeholders of England*

London: Printed and Sold by S. Keimer, 1715

ATTRIBUTION: Trent (*CHEL*); Hutchins, Moore, Novak.

Published on 22 January, this is an attack on Atterbury's anonymous High Tory polemic *English Advice to the Freeholders of England* (one of two such attacks attributed to Defoe, published within a day or two of each other – see **299**). It argues that Atterbury's accusations of Whig electoral corruption come ill from a party which plumbed new depths of corruption in the recent election, and that his equating of the Church (to which all well-disposed citizens wish well) with the Tory party is monstrous presumption. Plain country people can hardly be blamed for suspecting *all* Tories of disaffection and Jacobitism, after the late Tory débacle.

Nothing in the style or approach of this dullish tract immediately suggests Defoe, and it seems unlikely, *prima facie*, that he would have written the passage on p. 19 deprecating the electing of Dissenters to Parliament and rejoicing that so few are in fact ever elected, or indeed that he would have been so condemnatory of the late Harley administration. (See our note to **285**.)

293 The Immorality of the Priesthood

London: Printed for J. Roberts, 1715

ATTRIBUTION: Moore; Novak (as "Perhaps by Defoe").

Published in January 1715, and prompted by the King's recent "Injunctions" to the lower clergy not to meddle in state affairs, a raking-through of English history since the Reformation to demonstrate the factiousness and presumption of the High-Church clergy. The tract is nearly identical to *The Justice and Necessity of Restraining the Clergy* (**294**).

Pat Rogers argues convincingly in "Defoe and *The Immorality of the Priesthood*", *PBSA*, 67 (1973), 245–53, that this work is more likely to be by John Oldmixon.

294 The Justice and Necessity of Restraining the Clergy

London: Printed for J. Roberts, 1715

ATTRIBUTION: Moore.

Differs from **293** (*q.v.*) only by a different title-page and the lack of three preliminary leaves.

295 The Secret History of the Scepter

London: Printed and Sold by S. Keimer, 1715

ATTRIBUTION: Trent (*Nation*); Hutchins, Moore, Novak.

A temperate history of the rise of party management and faction in Britain since the time of Charles II, repeating as a refrain that all the famous disputes about "the Church in danger" and "toleration", in Anne's reign, were really no more than party-political contests as to who should gain possession of the *Sceptre*. It outlines the painful situation of Harley, left unable to clear his name if innocent, or to have his guilt firmly pronounced. Describes the "*Staff*" (i.e. White Staff) pamphlets as somewhat misleading.

The warning against the *White Staff* pamphlets (p. 58) inclines us to reject the attribution of this sensibly written but dullish pamphlet to Defoe.

296 The Secret History of State Intrigues

London: Printed and Sold by S. Keimer, 1715

ATTRIBUTION: Trent (*Nation*); Hutchins, Moore, Novak.

Identical to **295** (*q.v.*), apart from its title-page.

297 The Candidate

London: Printed and Sold by S. Keimer, 1715

ATTRIBUTION: Trent (Bibliography); Hutchins, Moore, Novak.

A rambling, partly facetious, diatribe against corrupt election practices, published in the election month of January 1715. It includes an act from a blank verse comedy, "written many years ago", about a wealthy citizen, ("the Regent of the Jobbing World"), his book-keeper and an Exchange broker.

The tract has a good deal of rather banal liveliness but never suggests Defoe; and the idea of Defoe, who often spoke with contempt of the theatre, presenting himself as a playwright, arouses one's scepticism. An unconvincing attribution.

299 A Reply to a Traiterous Libel, Entituled, *English Advice to the Freeholders of Great Britain*

London: Printed for J. Baker, 1715

ATTRIBUTION: Wilson (as bearing "strong marks of our author's pen"); Lee, Trent (*CHEL*), Hutchins, Moore, Novak.

An attack on Atterbury's *English Advice to the Freeholders of England* and published within a day or two of *Treason Detected* (**292**, *q.v.*). It argues that most of the steps that the author of *English Advice* prophesies that the Whigs will take (like fighting wars on behalf of Hanover, maintaining a standing army, repealing the Triennial Act, intensifying the campaign against the Church and renewing the war with France) are unlikely to happen, since they would simply not be in the Whigs' interest. Nor is his stress on King George's Lutheranism fair, for it is absurd to speak of Lutheranism as a threat on the scale of popery (was not Luther the "Morning Star of the Reformation"?), and anyway the King has entered into communion with the Church of England.

There seems no obvious reason to assign this unremarkable and heavy-handed pamphlet to Defoe. The simple-minded polemical style never calls him to mind; and, given his known "moderate" views on the standing army question, it would be hard to associate him with the argument used on p. 37, that the immediate result of a standing army would be military government.

300 The Protestant Jubilee

London: Printed and Sold by S. Keimer, 1715

ATTRIBUTION: Moore; Novak.

A rabid Whiggish mock-sermon, saying how plainly God has revealed his hand in the choosing of certain significant days, and especially 20 January, the day when Charles I was brought to trial and the one now appointed to celebrate the blessed accession of King George. Significance is drawn from the Queen having died on St. Bartholomew's Day and the Schism Act having (it is hoped) died with her. A savage attack is made on the "loathsome" measures of the late Tory adminstration in making a "treacherous Peace" (pp. 15–16), the "Malefactors" now awaiting punishment being likened to Guy Fawkes and his fellow-conspirators.

Despite the fact that Defoe sometimes let his fancy run on "significant" coincidences of dates, this wild anti-Harleyite farrago strikes one as a most implausible attribution.

301 A Letter to a Merry Young Gentleman

London: Sold by J. Morphew, 1715

ATTRIBUTION: Trent (*CHEL*); Hutchins, Moore, Novak.

A facetious rejoinder to Thomas Burnet's *The Necessity of Impeaching the Late Ministry: In a Letter to the Earl of Halifax*, which called for the blood of the late Tory ministers. It pretends to think that the author of this low production cannot really be the son of the revered Bishop Burnet and that it is a sort of *Shortest Way with the Dissenters* in reverse, i.e. a satire written by a High Tory to bring Whiggism into disrepute.

Trent points out in his Bibliography that a contemporaneous *Letter to Thomas Burnet, Esq.* seems to imply that *A Letter to a Merry Young Gentleman* is by William Oldisworth, editor of the Tory *Examiner*. Since the author of *A Letter to a Merry Young Gentleman* avowedly writes as a "moderate Tory", this is *prima facie* not an implausible attribution. Trent's reasons for rejecting it and ascribing the work to Defoe are based largely on his untrustworthy verbal "tests", there being no external evidence linking the work to him.

302 Burnet and Bradbury

London: Printed and Sold by S. Keimer, 1715

ATTRIBUTION: Crossley; Trent (*Nation*), Hutchins, Moore, Novak.

A somewhat furious remonstrance, written in the person of a member of the Church of England who claims to be "unacquainted with the Sects of Dissenters", against Thomas Burnet's *The Necessity of Impeaching the Late Ministry* and the *Sermon on the Late Thanksgiving* by the well-known Dissenting minister Thomas Bradbury – both of which call for the blood of the late Harley administration, saying that the people "EXPECT" it. This behaviour on the part of a Dissenting minister, says the tract, is directly against the King's recent "Injunctions" to the clergy not to meddle in politics, and it is a great injustice to Harley and his associates, who have not yet been accused of any specific crime. The tract complains of "the Injustice of Suffering the *Dissenting Preachers* thus to trample under their Feet, the Ministers of that Church, by whom they are indulged in the Liberties they shew themselves so unworthy to enjoy" (p. 8), and it hints that the Church may one day exact a just revenge.

Considering the passage just quoted, it would only be feasible to assign this tract to Defoe by a desperate resort to the "Defoe in disguise" theory, for which nothing in it offers grounds. An unconvincing attribution.

304 The Fears of the Pretender Turn'd into the Fears of Debauchery

London: Printed and Sold by S. Keimer, 1715

ATTRIBUTION: Crossley; Trent (*Nation*), Hutchins, Moore, Novak.

Published apparently about January 1715, a solemn lament that the immediate reponse to the glorious good fortune of King George's accession and the removal of all fears of the Pretender, has been, not thankfulness to Heaven, but a vogue for stage-plays and a contempt on the part of the nobility and Court for (as they call them) the "officious fanaticks" and "flattering Presbyterians" who helped to bring about this blessing. The King, though at present he encourages this fashion for the theatre, will surely soon realise how fatal it is to the British people. Richard Steele, for all the merits of his *Tatler* and *Spectator*, has done more than all the other "agents Hell ever employ'd before" to ruin Britain by encouraging this trend.

The heavily "pulpit" style of this tract and (for instance) the rather absurd remark on p. 27 that the present torrent of vice may bring down the grieving King to an early grave, do not suggest Defoe; and evidently the mere fact of his known hostility to the stage is no sufficient reason for ascribing this tract to him. Nor, in our view, is the reference to King William's injunction to "die in the last ditch" (p. 22), though this is one of which Defoe was fond.

306 Reflections upon Sacheverell's Sermons of January 20 and 31

London: Printed and Sold by A. Boulter, 1715

ATTRIBUTION: Moore; Novak ("Remarks, preface and postscript by Defoe").

An attack on Sacheverell in the form of a reprinting of his sermon on the anniversary of Charles I's execution, and of a summary of his sermon on 20 January, with a Preface and some severe Whiggish "Remarks".

Pat Rogers, in "Addenda and Corrigenda: Moore's *Checklist* of Defoe", *PBSA*, 75 (1981), 60–64, describes this as "Very probably the work of Oldmixon".

308 Some Reasons Offered by the Late Ministry in Defence of their Administration

London: Printed for J. Morphew, 1715

ATTRIBUTION: Trent (*Nation*); Hutchins, Moore, Novak (as "Probably by Defoe").

A lengthy and somewhat wooden recital of the standard arguments in defence of the late Tory ministry, under the pretence of an impartial report of what Harley and his associates say on their own behalf. It is one of a number of pamphlets prompted by Thomas Burnet's *The Necessity of Impeaching the Late Ministry* of February 1715. By comparison with the *White Staff* pamphlets, it is so clumsy and implausible a defence of the Harleyites (implying, for instance, that any suggestion that they could have had any dealings with the Pretender is merely ludicrous) that it would be hard to believe it by Defoe.

Trent ascribes it purely on internal evidence, of his usual verbal kind.

311 An Apology for the Army: In a Short Essay on Fortitude, etc.

London: Printed for J. Roberts, 1715

ATTRIBUTION: Trent (*CHEL*); Hutchins, Moore, Novak.

A diatribe, written in the person of an "Officer", against the current vilification or depreciation of the military virtues and against the treatment of the army by the late Tory administration: the ungenerosity to veterans, the disgrace of the "restraining orders" of 1712, etc.

Trent's commentary in his Bibliography is more than usually self-persuading. Despite the absence of some of Defoe's "stylistic peculiarities", he finds the ascription to him "imperative", since the author sounds more like a journalist than an army officer. Thus, if it is not the work of a real officer, "I naturally find its author in that contemporary pamphleteer most likely to disguise himself". The reason why Defoe should have written it was, he surmises, simply that he "caught at every opportunity in the year 1715 to employ his pen and to give proof of his repentance for the part he played under the late ministry".

It is a puzzle why subsequent bibliographers should have taken over this fanciful attribution of Trent's without query. It would be easy to find arguments against Defoe's authorship, but the irrationality of Trent's case makes this unnecessary.

313 Some Methods to Supply the Defects of the Late Peace

London: Printed for J. Baker [1715]

ATTRIBUTION: Crossley; Trent (*Nation*), Hutchins, Moore, Novak.

Argues that the important thing in the present situation is to restore Britain's influence abroad, so that "our Words shall be as loud as our Cannon" (p. 18), and the only way to achieve this is by peace and union at home: at present Britons are "biting" one another at a horrible rate. The cry of "the Church in Danger" is absurd, for the King well knows that the Church is his main support.

A passage on pp. 9–13 argues at length that Britain's "great business" at present is to enforce the demolition of Dunkirk – both its port and harbour. This contrasts so markedly with the position taken up by Defoe earlier in *Mercator* (see 4–6 February 1714) and adopted in *Reasons concerning the Immediate Demolishing of Dunkirk* (1713), which there is reason to think is probably by him – i.e. that, since Dunkirk is now officially in Britain's possession, it will be of more advantage to her *un*destroyed – as to cast serious doubts on this attribution. See also *A General History of Trade* (1713), p. 37, where a plea is made against destroying Dunkirk as a port.

314 A Remonstrance from Some Country Whigs to a Member of a Secret Committee

London: Printed for J. Morphew, 1715

ATTRIBUTION: Trent (*CHEL*); Hutchins, Moore, Novak (as "Probably by Defoe").

The "Country Whigs" list all the wicked activities of which rumour (no doubt rightly) accuses the late Tory ministers, but they expatiate on the virtues which they "EXPECT" the Secret Committee to display: indifference to public clamour, due process of law, no working off of party enmities or attempts to appease foreign powers.

The repeated play on the word "EXPECT" is presumably a satirical allusion to the use of the same word in recent Whiggish tracts by Thomas Bradbury, Burnet and Steele, but otherwise one does not detect much satire; and despite the plea for a fair trial, the anti-Harleyite line adopted is so much at odds with the *White Staff* defences of Harley (see our note on **285**) as to give little grounds for supposing Defoe to be the author.

*315 The Happiness of the Hanover Succession

London: Printed and Sold by S. Keimer, 1715

ATTRIBUTION: Moore (as "Very probably, not certainly Defoe's"); Novak (as "Perhaps by Defoe").

A flaming attack on the late Harley administration, explicitly repudiating the *White Staff* pamphlets ("however the *Secret Historian* may endeavour to paint the Devil *White*") and depicting Harley as "a Person, that without Remorse, basely Sacrificed his Principles to his Interest, and by an unbridled Ambition guided, trampled down publick Good in his Way to Preferment" (p. 8). Ends with a paean of praise for the Hanoverian dispensation and a vision of the entire Tory party making a humble confession of its sins.

Moore notes: "If it is Defoe's, it is an example of a tract written for the new ministry, but slanted so as to do the Earl of Oxford no real harm".

A particularly wild attribution (especially in asserting that the tract could do Harley "no real harm").

316 An Attempt towards a Coalition of English Protestants

London: Printed and Sold by J. Roberts, 1715

ATTRIBUTION: Trent (*Nation*; but not in his Bibliography); Hutchins, Moore, Novak.

A well-written piece, presumably composed before the 1715 Rising, saying that there must be an end to recriminations over the past (one party has probably been as bad as another); political preaching must be restrained; political pamphleteering ought to be suppressed; and the Dissenters ought to be granted civil liberty, in return for which they would gladly grant "regency" to the Church of England.

The style of this never suggests Defoe, and certain of its sentiments argue against his authorship: i.e. the assertion (p. 8) that atheists can be excellent citizens (in his known writings his liberalism does not extend to atheists); and the recommendation (p. 22) that there should be a legal ban on political pamphleeering (his customary view was that pamphleteers should be free to publish though must expect to be held legally responsible for what they wrote). The suggestions about the Dissenters also do not reflect his own strong and idiosyncratic views. The only piece of evidence suggesting him is the line "For all Men wou'd be Emp'rors if they could" (p. 32), which is an adaptation of a well-known line in *The True-Born Englishman* (and *Jure Divino*); but it would not be safe to build much on this.

316a An Account of the Riots, Tumults, and Other Treasonable Practices: Since His Majesty's Accession to the Throne

London: Printed for J. Baker, 1715

ATTRIBUTION: Moore.

A late attribution by Moore: the tract is largely composed of letters from various parts of the country reporting anti-Hanoverian riots on Coronation Day (1714) and Election Day (1715). It calls for a strengthening of the law against such disturbances.

Moore describes the contents as "a succession of ostensible letters (edited or rewritten by Defoe)", adding "See also Nos. **286** and **288**". He does not explain why he supposes Defoe had a hand in them, and **286** and **288** (*qq.v.*) are now thought to be by Oldmixon.

318 His Majesty's Obligations to the Whigs

London: Printed for J. Baker, 1715

ATTRIBUTION: Moore; Novak (as "Probably by Defoe").

Published in early June, a scornful and satirical attack on the Tories for complaining at being left out of the present administration. (What possible claims can they make on the King's friendship?) It dismisses the argument brought (by "an able Writer for the late Ministry") in the *White Staff* pamphlets, that Harley and the Tories were playing a double game with the Jacobites: on the contrary, it says, they were all too sincere in their promises to the Pretender (pp. 22–23).

The repudiation of the *White Staff* pamphlets makes this an unlikely attribution to Defoe. (See our note on **285**.)

319 A Brief History of the Pacifick Campaign ... By an Officer in the Army

London: Printed for J. Baker, 1715

ATTRIBUTION: Moore; Novak.

A wholesale attack on the business of the secret "restraining orders" given to Ormonde during the campaign of 1712, and on the double-dealing of the British with their Allies. It refers to Stanhope's declaration that he could bring documentary evidence to prove British complicity with the French – a fact which seems to date this tract to March 1715. It argues that this proof is all that is lacking to support a charge of high treason against the Tory leaders.

The uncompromising severity against the late Harley administration argues against Defoe's authorship. (See our note on **285**.)

320 Some Considerations on the Danger of the Church

London: Printed and Sold by J. Roberts, J. Harrison, and A. Dod, 1715

ATTRIBUTION: Crossley (who, however, went back on the attribution later); Trent (*Nation*), Hutchins, Moore, Novak.

A commonplace disquisition on the theme that, if "the Church is in danger", this danger comes from within – i.e. from the persecuting ways and restless disloyalty of the high-flying clergy.

The sentiments, apart from the attack on the Treaty of Commerce, are ones that Defoe would have endorsed, but no more so than a dozen other writers, so there seems no particular reason to attribute this to him. (Trent thought Defoe's authorship was "strongly suggested" by the style, though it had been somewhat disguised to suit the dignity of a Churchman addressing Convocation.)

320a A Letter from a Gentleman of the Church of England to All the High-Flyers of Great-Britain

Dublin: Reprinted and Sold by Thomas Humes, 1716

ATTRIBUTION: Moore; Novak.

A vehement pulpit-style attack on the high-flyers by a professed member of the Church of England. It is because of the high-flyers, the author says, that the "Church is in danger", and not because of the Dissenters, who have behaved in a dutiful and loyal manner. Is the Church endangered by the dismissal of a set of men who, when in office, were "*Secret Traytors*", and who are now "*Open Rebels*"? No, the danger to the Church comes from within.

Moore comments, in "Defoe Acquisitions at the Huntington Library", *HLQ*, 28 (1964), 45–57, "Its fault is not that it is not easily identifiable as Defoe's, but rather that it is so characteristic of him that it says little that cannot be found elsewhere in his writings"; and he lists five supposedly cognate tracts – **316**, **331**, **338**, **352**, **366**. We have marked **316**, **331** and **366** for de-attribution, and in any event **316** is utterly different in tone and style from the present work. Moore's article on these recent acquisitions at the Huntington, of which he attributed to Defoe for the first time no less than eight, as well as identifying two more as earlier versions of tracts already so attributed, strikes us as a careless and altogether over-confident performance. To his remark that the present work "says little that cannot be found elsewhere in his [Defoe's] writings", it would probably be fair to add, "or in the writings of a score of his contemporaries".

The weakness of Moore's case for the present attribution, and the general style and anti-Harleyite tendency of the tract, seem to us reasons for rejection.

321 An Humble Address to Our Soveraign Lord the People

London: Printed for J. Baker, 1715

ATTRIBUTION: Crossley; Trent (*Nation*), Hutchins, Moore, Novak.

A vigorous appeal, in the person of a High-Church man, to the "High-Church mobs", telling them they are the plaything of dangerous Jacobite incendiaries and, if they do not cease from rioting, will bring destruction on themselves, if not on the country. The author, a supporter of divine right, says that he and his like would gladly abolish the toleration granted to Dissenters, but that they would not therefore think it right to demolish Dissenting meeting-houses. Such mob violence by "Our Soveraign Lord the People", can only help the Pretender.

Crossley gives no reason for making this attribution to Defoe; and Trent, who can offer no logical explanation for Defoe's wanting to write such a pamphlet, which neither expresses his own views nor can be interpreted as a lampoon, falls back on the theory that "we have here one of the pamphlets needed to make up a full bale of work for so indefatigable a writer as Defoe during the somewhat barren summer and fall of 1715".

322 The History of the Wars, of His Present Majesty Charles XII King of Sweden ... By a Scots Gentleman in the Sweedish Service

London. Printed for A. Bell, T. Varnam, J. Osborn, W. Taylor and J. Baker, 1715

ATTRIBUTION: Lee; Trent (*Nation*), Hutchins, Moore, Novak.

An immensely detailed 400-page "campaign history" or chronicle of the wars of Charles XII, giving the impression of being the work of an inexperienced writer. We argue the improbability of its being by Defoe, and discuss the "snowball" effect of this attribution of Lee's, in *Canonisation*, pp. 17–28.

Paula Backscheider has found evidence, in the form of an advertisement in the *Weekly Packet*, 9–16 July 1715, for the interesting fact that the *History of the Wars of Charles XII* was commissioned by the Emperor. (See *Daniel Defoe: His Life* [Baltimore and London, 1989], p. 592.) She contests our negative view of the attribution, as presented in the *Canonisation*, arguing that there are many parallels between the *History* and comments on Sweden in the *Review*, but we cannot say that we find these at all striking. To her comment that we "offer no concrete evidence" for our view (and "suggest no other author") it has, of course, to be answered that no concrete evidence has ever been brought *for* the attribution.

324a Hanover or Rome

London: Printed for J. Roberts, 1715

ATTRIBUTION: Moore; Novak.

A furious Whiggish tract which, though listed in the *Monthly Catalogue* for July, seems to have been published after the Earl of Ormonde's flight on 8 August 1715. It argues that there is not a shred of credibility in the Jacobite case and that no person in his right mind can doubt that Harley, Bolingbroke and Harcourt were "His Majesty's Enemies" and friends to the Pretender, as revealed in their "scandalous and ruinous Peace" (p. 21). Hence, in the present crisis and threat of invasion, the King must unquestionably be allowed to raise a substantial army.

Considering the severity of the attacks on Harley (see also pp. 29–31), one would not instantly think that this diatribe was by Defoe. The only piece of evidence brought forward by Moore in support of his attribution is the inclusion on the final page of an anecdote about a Cromwellian officer encouraging his men with the cry "Come on my Men, they Blaspheme, the Day is our own". (See his article, "Defoe Acquisitions at the Huntington Library", *HLQ*, 28 [1964], 45–57.) Defoe was unquestionably fond of this anecdote, but on its own it does not seem enough to persuade one to accept such an otherwise unlikely attribution.

327 The Traiterous and Foolish Manifesto of the Scots Rebels

London: Printed and Sold by R. Burleigh, 1715

ATTRIBUTION: Trent (*Nation*); Hutchins, Moore, Novak.

A paragraph-by-paragraph attack on the "Scots Manifesto" issued by the Jacobite rebels in October 1715. It derides the praise currently bestowed on the style of the Manifesto and argues that the Earl of Mar's views and conduct are self-contradictory (he complains of the Union but was one of the chief agents in its creation). It asks, since the Manifesto complains of the treatment of Scottish troops by the Dutch, whether the rebels want a war with the Dutch, to ruin Britain economically? At one point (p. 17) it refuses to reproduce the words of the Manifesto, as too wickedly traitorous.

Everything in this competent and sensible pamphlet seems broadly consonant with Defoe's views and it would be perfectly possible to imagine it as by him. On the other hand nothing in the way of external evidence, nor any quality in the prose style, actually point directly to him, so that it seems to belong in the "possible" rather than "probable" category.

328 Bold Advice: or, Proposals for the Entire Rooting out of Jacobitism

London: Printed by J. Moor, 1715

ATTRIBUTION: Trent (*Nation*); Hutchins, Novak (as "Almost certainly by Defoe").

A very "hot" piece, telling the Government (in dictatorial fashion) that now is the moment, when the Jacobite cause is so much weakened by the accession of George I, to stamp out Jacobitism altogether, by imposing an oath of abjuration on every citizen and penalising those who refuse to take it by taxes, bail, an annual check on any firearms in their possession, and if necessary banishment. The "Adviser" speaks severely of the crimes of the "late Managers", and he says it must be made a criminal offence for the clergy to preach politics from the pulpit. A reference to the King's forthcoming "Injunctions" to the lower clergy (p. 40) dates the writing of this to December 1714.

The dictatorial tone and the wild unrealism of its schemes make this unlikely to be by Defoe.

329 An Address to the People of England: Shewing the Unworthiness of their Behaviour to King George

London: Printed for J. Wyat, 1715

ATTRIBUTION: Moore; Novak (as "Perhaps by Defoe").

A platitudinous quasi-sermon, in the person of a member of the Church of England, against the follies of High-Church doctrines ("indefeasible hereditary right", etc.) and the attempt to blame the Rebellion on a too great tolerance towards Dissenters. It urges its readers to "shew ourselves zealous to assert the ancient Glory of the *Church of England*" and speaks complacently of the "Bill against Occasional Conformity, so much longed for". It defends George I from the charge of breaking the Constitution by governing through a standing army and ends with a fulsome panegyric of him.

Moore presumably supposed this to be a case of Defoe disguising himself as a Churchman, but it is hard to see on what grounds.

331 A Letter from One Clergy-Man to Another, upon the Subject of the Rebellion

London: Printed for John Baker, 1716 [for 1715]

ATTRIBUTION: Trent (*CHEL*); Hutchins, Moore, Novak (as "Probably by Defoe").

A bumbling and parsonical tract asking (in a series of "Socratic" questions) whether it is not very unjust to suspect George I of dangerous designs on the Church merely because he displays low-Church sympathies. It blames the present rebellion on dissensions among the clergy and eulogises the King warmly.

Trent assigned this on the basis of style and of the fact that the author recommends to his fellow-clergyman a tract which he refers to as *The Best Method of Supplying the Defects of the Late Peace* (evidently a misnomer for *Some Methods to Supply the Defects of the Late Peace* (1715) (Moore, **313**). (In his comments on **313** Trent writes: "when I find one of his tracts 'puffed' in another pamphlet, I am immediately tempted to add the latter item to his bibliography if I possibly can".) Moore, speaking of the present work, comments that "Defoe disguised his style to a large extent, to make this tract pass as the work of a clergyman of the Church of England" but claims that it contains "several characteristic idioms and allusions", though he does not specify them. Also, like Trent, he draws support from the complimentary reference to **313**. This latter (*q.v.*), however, is an item we regard as questionable also. All in all, the case for the present attribution seems weak and relies too much on the "Defoe in disguise" theory.

331a A Conference with a Jacobite

London: Printed for J. Baker and T. Warner, 1716

ATTRIBUTION: Moore.

A dialogue between a country clergyman and a Jacobite parishioner, in which the "Gentleman" pretends to sympathise with the Parson for taking the Oaths of Allegiance and Abjuration out of necessity and against his better conscience, causing the Parson to deny the charge with indignation, telling the Gentleman how sacrosanct oaths were even in pagan antiquity. The Gentleman asks him how he can defend defrauding the legitimate king of Great Britain of his rights, to which the Parson replies that even if the Pretender were James II's genuine offspring, which is by no means certain, his claims to the throne under common law had been limited by statute. The Gentleman, impressed, agrees to consider the clergyman's arguments and hopes they can talk again.

This somewhat naive dialogue, unrelieved by characterisation or wit, does not at all suggest the Defoe of *The Family Instructor* etc., and Moore's comment that it is "Strikingly similar to No. **331** in argument" is no help to the ascription, since **331** (*A Letter from One Clergy-Man to Another*) (*q.v.*) seems unlikely to be by Defoe either – partly for the same reasons.

332 [Letter from General Forster to the Earl of Mar]

[1715]

ATTRIBUTION: Moore.

A fictitious letter from the Jacobite rebel General Forster to the Earl of Mar, dated "From my *Head Quarters* at *Newgate*, Dec. 9. 1715", reporting how his troops have made a triumphal march to London and taken up quarters in the Marshalsea and elsewhere. He tells Mar of their joy at hearing of his great victory at Dumblain. A postscript runs: "The publishing of this Account of our Victory by Mr. *Freebairn*, the King's Printer at Perth, will I doubt not, be as satisfactory to Friends there, as his publishing of yours, was to Friends here, since they are equally true, and I will take Care to have them re-publish'd with Advantage, by Friend *Keimer*, and *D.F.* his *Amanuensis*, in the *London Post*."

Boyer prints this letter "for the Humour of it" in the *Political State* for December 1715. It also appeared (without comment) in the *Flying-Post* for 17–20 December 1715.

Moore, in "Defoe's Hand in *A Journal of the Earl of Marr's Proceedings*", *HLQ*, 17 (1954), 209–28, refers to this as "the most amusing of all his [Defoe's] attacks on Mar" but suggests no reason why it should be ascribed to him. It is not absolutely clear what the point of the reference to "D.F.", in the Postscript, is, though it is not impossible that Defoe had some association with Keimer's *London Post*. We have, moreover, not been able to discover whether the letter was in fact printed in the *London Post*. However, the joke about "D.F." as Keimer's "Amanuensis" does not particularly strike one as grounds for attributing the *Letter* to him.

333 Proper Lessons for the Tories

London: Printed and Sold by J. Roberts, 1716

ATTRIBUTION: Moore (initially as "Probably, not certainly Defoe's", but in the Second Supplement, p. 249, as "Certainly Defoe's"); Novak (as "Almost certainly by Defoe").

Published in May 1716, a mock biblical narrative, pretendedly designed to be read on stated days throughout the year, of the overthrowing of James II, who "went a whoring after strange Gods", and of the Jacobite cause under Queen Anne. Chapter 8, "verses" xx-xxxi, tells how the Tories "sold their Country", "betray'd the Nation", were "paving the Way to bring in Idolatry" and accepted bribes from the "Gauls".

Moore, in "Defoe Acquisitions at the Huntington Library", *HLQ,* 28 (1964), 45–57, argues that there was an earlier version of this tract entitled *Proper Lessons Written by a Quaker*, and that this explains the biblical style and renders the attribution to Defoe more certain. However, it cannot be said that the work much resembles Defoe's known "Quaker" tracts, and the savage attack on the Harley ministry seems unlikely to have come from Defoe's pen (see our note on **285**).

334 Some Account of the Two Nights Court at Greenwich

London: Printed for J. Baker, 1716

ATTRIBUTION: Boyer; Chalmers (as "Supposed to be De Foe's"), Wilson (who says however that "It was probably the work of some zealous Whig"), Lee, Trent (*CHEL*), Hutchins, Moore, Novak.

A "secret history" of the disarray and treasonable conspiracies of some members of the late Tory ministry following the unexpected death of Queen Anne. Speeches made during their meetings at Greenwich on the evening and day following King George's arrival in England are reported at length by an author who believes that the recent rebellion can be traced back to them.

This is an instructive example of how a work, once attributed, can remain in an author's canon by sheer inertia. Boyer's attribution clearly led to Chalmers's inclusion of it in his "Supposed" category. Wilson, in turn, though obviously doubting Defoe's authorship, nevertheless included it in his list, and it has been retained without question by all subsequent bibliographers. It is, in fact, a pretty feeble piece, in which the dialogue and debates are all conducted in platitudes and generalities, and completely lacking the comedy and satirical bite of a work like *The Secret History of the October Club* (1711), which is very probably by Defoe.

The only piece of evidence which might suggest Defoe is a remark by one of the speakers that "the Hearts of Subjects are the Glory and the Strength of Kings" (p. 64). This is very close to a line in Defoe's poem *The Mock Mourners*, line 159: "And Hearts of Subjects are the strength of Kings". However, the allusion, if it is one, could admit of various explanations, and by itself is insufficient to persuade one that the work must have been written by Defoe.

335 The Case of the Protestant Dissenters in England Fairly Stated

London: Printed for R. Ford and Sold by J. Roberts and J. Harrison, 1716

ATTRIBUTION: Moore; Novak (as "Perhaps by Defoe").

Published in January 1716, a vigorous statement of the grievances of the Dissenters and of the inequity of any discrimination against citizens (apart from atheists and Papists) on grounds of religion. It argues that the 1715 rising came about because Dissenters, the great supporters of the Hanoverian succession, were excluded from the running of the country.

Through continual exposition, Defoe's idiosyncratic though coherent line on the question of the Dissenters is sufficiently familiar to the reader for it to be reasonable to doubt his authorship of any pamphlet, like the present one, which expresses a different one. The personal attack on Harley on p. 14 also seems unlikely to have come from him. (It is to be remembered that, as often, no case has been made *for* the attribution.)

336 The Address of the Episcopal Clergy ... of Aberdeen to the Pretender: With Remarks

[1716]

ATTRIBUTION: Moore; Novak (as "Attributed by J.R. Moore").

This reprints the Address of welcome delivered by the episcopal clergy of Aberdeen to the Pretender, on 26 December 1715, adding some caustic remarks on the covert popery of the episcopal clergy and on the behaviour of the Pretender himself.

Moore notes that this "Address", as well as the "Address" of the Magistrates and Town Council of Aberdeen (see **337**), was also reprinted in *Annals of King George, Year the Third* (1718) (**385**) – a work which he, again, was the first to ascribe to Defoe, and it looks as though this might be why he made the present attribution. We find his case for ascribing the *Annals* to Defoe unsatisfactory (see our note on **351**) and therefore no support to the present ascription. Further, one of the "Remarks" in the present tract, to the effect that the Harley ministry "thought it in their Interest to encourage these Nurseries of Jacobitism", does not seem likely to have come from Defoe. It should be added that the reprint of the "Address" to which Moore refers is in fact in *Annals of King George, Year the Second* (1717) (**351**); see Appendix No. U, pp. 65–66 (separately paginated).

337 The Address of the Magistrates and Town Council of Aberdeen, to the Pretender: With Remarks

[1716]

ATTRIBUTION: Moore; Novak (as "Attributed by J.R. Moore").

This gives the text of the Address by the Magistrates and Town Council of Aberdeen welcoming the Pretender, followed by censorious comments. See note on **336**, above.

*339 The Declaration of the Free-Holders of Great Britain

[1716]

ATTRIBUTION: Moore (as "Probably, not certainly, by Defoe"); Novak (as "Attributed tentatively by J.R. Moore").

An answer to the Pretender's recent "Declaration", denying his accusations that the royal family are "*Aliens to our Country*" and "*Strangers to our Language*", and that George I plans to subordinate Britain's interests to those of Hanover. It ridicules the benefits which the Pretender promises to bring to the British people.

Moore offers no evidence in support of this tentative ascription, and it is hard to guess what led him to make it, nothing in it pointing at all obviously to Defoe.

341 An Account of the Proceedings against the Rebels ... Published from an Original Manuscript

London: Printed for J. Baker and Tho. Warner, 1716

ATTRIBUTION: Moore; Novak.

An account of the severities meted out to the defeated rebels after Monmouth's rebellion and to the Scottish and Irish rebels at the same period, with the aim of showing, by comparison, the weakness of the 1715 rebels' cause and the injustice of accusing George I of harshness towards them.

One is at a loss to know why Moore should have supposed this laborious historical compilation, stuffed with the minor details of events of thirty years before, to be by Defoe.

342 The Proceedings of the Government against the Rebels

[1716]

ATTRIBUTION: Moore; Novak.

A brief abstract of **341**, *q.v.*

343 Remarks on the Speech of James Late Earl of Derwentwater

London, Printed for R. Burleigh, 1716

ATTRIBUTION: Moore (as "Very probably, not certainly, Defoe's"; in the Second Supplement as "Certainly Defoe's"); Novak (as "Perhaps by Defoe").

A paragraph by paragraph analysis of the Earl of Derwentwater's speech at the scaffold on 24 February, with uncharitable moralisings and reflections on the wickedness of Jesuit principles.

Moore fails to explain why he suspected, and later (see "Second Supplement", p. 249), grew confident that this was by Defoe.

346 The Ill Consequences of Repealing the Triennial Act: In a Letter to Mr. Sh[ippc]n

London: Printed for J. Baker and T. Warner, 1716

ATTRIBUTION: Moore; Novak (as "Probably by Defoe").

A neat anti-Jacobite satire, in which a Jacobite conspirator suggests to the High Tory William Shippen some arguments which he could use to his circle of friends and to the public against the threatened repeal of the Triennial Act – providing the reader, who will read it in reverse, with good grounds for supporting the repeal. Contains some nice ironic touches. It occurs to one to wonder whether the tract is not actually drawing on Shippen's speech in the Commons debate on 24 April 1716, in which he used some of those very arguments, and that the date ("9 April") which is given in the tract itself and which Moore treats as the date of publication could be false, the ante-dating being meant to give the tract an air of prophecy.

One would not at all rule out Defoe as the author of this, but it is hard to make out any definite case for connecting him with it.

347 A Dialogue between a Whig and a Jacobite upon the Subject of the Late Rebellion

London: Printed for J. Roberts, 1716

ATTRIBUTION: Moore; Novak (as "Probably by Defoe").

A hackneyed debate, occasioned by the execution of the rebel Jacobite lords on 6 March 1716, in which the Whig recites all the familiar arguments, historical and political, against the Jacobite rebels' cause and eventually causes the Jacobite to say he has been made to see matters differently.

One can imagine no sound reason for assigning this tract, which is devoid of wit and characterisation, to Defoe.

348 A True Account of the Proceedings at Perth

London: Printed for J. Baker, 1716

ATTRIBUTION: Crossley; Trent, Hutchins, Moore, Novak.

A vivid account of the arrival of the Pretender at Perth during the later stages of the 1715 Rising, and of the Highlanders' disappointment with him and with their leader the Earl of Mar's refusal to engage the English forces.

This tract, treated from the outset as an authentic historical document, was for long attributed to the Master of Sinclair. However, with the publication of his *Memoirs of the Rising* in 1858, it became evident that he was unlikely to be the author – for one thing, because he was not actually present in Perth during the period described. Crossley's ascription of the work to Defoe logically signified that it was to be regarded as fiction rather than fact (though this has not prevented subsequent historians of the Rising from continuing to draw on it as a genuine eye-witness account), and close inspection reveals that it is a clever piece of Whiggish Government propaganda, designed to support the repeal of the Triennial Act. Moore's case for Defoe's authorship involves a chain of mutually-supporting attributions, including *Annals of King George*, the Introduction to *A Journal of the Earl of Marr's Proceedings* and *History of the Reign of King George* and may be seen to be fatally circular. See further our article, "*A True Account of the Proceedings at Perth*: the Impact of an Historical Novel", *Eighteenth-Century Fiction*, 6 (1994), 233–42.

349 A Journal of the Earl of Marr's Proceedings

London: Reprinted and Sold by J. Baker [1716]

ATTRIBUTION: Trent (Bibliography); Moore, Novak.

An apologia for the failure of the 1715 Rising, compiled on behalf of the Earl of Mar and first published in Avignon in April 1716 as *A Letter from an Officer in the King's Army to his Friend in England*. (It was also translated into French, German and Spanish.) The present tract is a reprint published a month or two later in London, with a contemptuous Introduction exposing the incompetence and deceit of Mar's whole enterprise, thereby converting it into a piece of anti-Jacobite propaganda.

Moore, in "Defoe's Hand in *A Journal of the Earl of Marr's Proceedings*", *HLQ*, 17 (1954), 209–28 (a lengthy account of the compiling of the *Journal*), ascribes the Introduction to Defoe, though offering no grounds for this, and it forms a link in the chain of attributions discussed in our article cited in the preceding entry (**348**). Trent reports that he was alerted to a possible connection between Defoe and the *Journal* by a bookseller's catalogue in 1926.

350 Remarks on the Speeches of William Paul, Clerk, and John Hall of Otterburn, Esq.

London: Printed for J. Baker and T. Warner, 1716

ATTRIBUTION: Trent (*CHEL*); Hutchins, Moore, Novak.

A vindictive commentary on the dying speeches of two Jacobite rebels, executed in July 1716.

Trent makes the attribution on the basis of his verbal "tests", which he regarded as clinched by a curious reference on p. 8 to "the She-Comedian, who acted *Roxellana*" in the reign of Charles II (i.e. Hester Davenport, famous as Roxolana in Davenant's *Siege of Rhodes*). Nothing obviously supports the attribution (the "Roxellana" allusion being negligible), and a condemnatory reference to the late Harley ministry as having "betray'd the *Catalans*" argues a little against it.

351 The Annals of King George, Year the Second

London: Printed for A. Bell, W. Taylor and J. Baker, 1717

ATTRIBUTION: Trent (Bibliography); Moore, Novak (as "Written in part and ed. Defoe").

Published actually in October 1716, a lengthy chronicle of the year beginning August 1715, largely devoted to what it terms "a compleat History of the REBELLION". The work, with its numerous Appendixes, runs to over 450 pages and forms the second volume of an annual series which ran until 1721. It is Moore's claim that Defoe was responsible for it and for its successor, *The Annals of King George, Year the Third* (**385**). His note in the *Checklist* runs:

> For Volumes II and III of the *Annals* Defoe wrote at least the account of the Jacobite Rising and the military campaigns (singled out for special remark in the Preface to Volume II). This account is in Defoe's characteristic style, it overlaps many of his pamphlets on the subject, and it was borrowed from extensively by Defoe in his later work called *The History of the Reign of King George* [**407**, *q.v.*].

Volume III, unlike the present volume, covers a wide variety of current topics, and it will be convenient to discuss it here as well.

As may be seen, one is confronted here with a concatenation of first-time attributions, each supposedly supporting the others – a dubious procedure in bibliography. We examine the whole group of ascriptions, which includes one or two further items, in our article "*A True Account of the Proceedings at Perth*: The Impact of an Historical Novel", *Eighteenth-Century Fiction*, 6 (1994), 233–42. One of the pamphlets dealing with the 1715 Rising which Moore believes to be closely related to the *Annals, Year the Second* is *A True Account of the Proceedings at Perth* (**348**, *q.v.*). We do not in fact think the case for ascribing this to Defoe is proven; but further, though it is evident that the compiler of the *Annals, Year the Second* has read the *True Account*, for he borrows a phrase or two from it, he noticeably fails to make use of what is really significant in that striking pamphlet, which would suggest that he was not its author.

In *Annals of King George, Year the Third* one is at a loss to find anything definitely pointing to Defoe at all. The work takes a squarely pro-Government point of view and differs from *Mercurius Politicus*, with which Defoe is known to have been involved, in taking a hostile attitude towards the "defection" of Townshend and Walpole from their Whig colleagues in April 1717 (see, e.g., p. 114), and in wholeheartedly supporting Bishop Hoadly in the Bangorian controversy (see, e.g., p. 263). That Defoe could have been writing on both sides is, of course, perfectly possible in theory but, evidently, not in itself a reason for arguing that he did so.

The Tory-inclined *History of the Reign of King George* (1719) (**407**, *q.v.*), mentioned by Moore, makes extensive borrowings from the *Annals* and at one point (p. 203) says that it has drawn on Whig histories "and even in their very words", evidently implying that this shows good faith on the part of a Tory work. Elsewhere it gives the story a more Tory slant. Presumably Moore sees here merely a charade on Defoe's part, but the same objection arises, what is the evidence that justifies this?

353 Secret Memoirs of the New Treaty of Alliance with France

London: Printed and Sold by J. Roberts, 1716

ATTRIBUTION: Trent (*CHEL*); Hutchins, Moore, Novak.

An ingenious and subtle piece of pretended "secret history", written as by a Frenchman to a friend in England and purporting to depict the devious reasonings underlying the French Regent's statesmanlike decision to join in an alliance with Britain (the Triple Alliance). The occasion is taken for some mild irony at the expense of the British: their demagogic tendencies and "impetuous, implacable and revengeful" character. The account of the disputes between the various factions in France is vivid and knowledgeable and has some nice character-strokes. It is not easy to detect any definite political intention in the tract, except (by giving Machiavellian reasons why the treaty will benefit both France and Britain) to give general support to Stanhope and Sunderland in their, now completed, negotiations.

One could easily imagine this tract, which has some similarities to *Minutes of the Negotiations of Monsr. Mesnager* (1717), to be by Defoe, but it is hard to find anything which definitely points in his direction.

357 Faction in Power: or, The Mischiefs and Dangers of a High-Church Magistracy

London: Printed for R. Burleigh, 1717

ATTRIBUTION: Moore; Novak (as "Probably by Defoe").

Published in January 1717, a bellicose extreme-Whig tract urging the King and Government to purge corporations and the commission of peace of Tories, who, to a man, are Jacobites and enemies of the Hanoverian succession ("that every *Tory* is an Enemy to his Country, is as certain as that every *Tory* is a *Jacobite*", p. 47). The author of this rancorous tract describes himself as a member of the Church of England but attacks the laws against the Dissenters, who, he says, are often the most sober and thriving members of the community.

We know of no evidence to support this implausible attribution.

358 An Impartial Enquiry into the Conduct of ... Lord Viscount T[ownshend]

London: Printed for A. Dodd, 1717

ATTRIBUTION: Boyer; Trent (*CHEL*); Hutchins, Moore, Novak.

Published in early February 1717, a long and very wordy defence of Townshend, recently dismissed as Secretary of State, against the charges of mishandling the Barrier Treaty of 1709 and of undue harshness in the aftermath of the 1715 rebellion. It says that the King can bear him no personal ill-will, since he has made him Lord Lieutenant of Ireland and remarks (with evident reference to Toland's *State-Anatomy* of January 1717) that "It will no more be wondred, that some are willing to have Foreigners admitted into Places, Honours, Profits, etc. Seeing *Great Britain's* Great Men, her Counsellors and Nobility, seem to be so disconcerted in Interest, and divided among themselves, that none knows whether their Country may not stand in need of the Help of a better chosen Set of Men" (p. 75).

The prose style of this pamphlet, with its elaborate "periodic" sentences, is not suggestive of Defoe, nor is (for instance) the simple-minded praise of Dutch "Openness and Candour" (p. 17) – Defoe's normal attitude towards the Dutch being that they were indispensable allies but cunning and rapacious competitors. Altogether, one would need more evidence to assign this to Defoe with any confidence.

359 An Argument Proving that the Design of Employing and Enobling Foreigners is a Treasonable Conspiracy

London: Printed for the Booksellers of London and Westminster, 1717

ATTRIBUTION: Boyer, in *Political State*, February 1717, pp. 142–43; Trent (*Nation*), Hutchins, Moore, Novak.

On 21 January 1717 John Toland published *The State-Anatomy of Great Britain*, giving, as the title-page put it, "a Particular account of its [Britain's] several Interests and Parties ... and what each of them ... may hope or fear from the Reign and Family of King George". This treatise, designed to catch the attention of the King who had returned from Hanover two days before, proposed that Non-Jurors should be banished from the country, that the King's German ministers Baron Bernstorff and Baron Bothmar should, in violation of the Act of Settlement of 1701, be given English peerages, and that the King should be encouraged to keep a sizeable peacetime army.

The present tract, published on 11 February, expresses amazement at the arrogance of the author of the *State-Anatomy* in presuming to dictate to the House of Lords, and in suggesting schemes for "prostituting the illustrious Blood of our Nobility", and it speaks with horror of the insidious design to introduce a standing army in peacetime. The whole affair, it asserts, must be a conspiracy of "a Sett of selfish and designing Men" (by implication the now dominant faction of Sunderland, Stanhope and the King's German ministers) who, fearing exposure by "some honest and loyal Patriots, who yet remain in the Administration" (by implication

Townshend and Walpole and their supporters) have made use of Toland
to test the temperature of the nation.

The *Argument* prompted Abel Boyer, Defoe's bitter enemy, to accuse
Defoe of its authorship and to point out, gleefully, the gross inconsistency
between the pamphlet's appeal to purity of "blood" and scaremongering
about standing armies and Defoe's earlier sentiments as expressed in *The
True-Born Englishman* and *An Argument Shewing, that a Standing Army, with
Consent of Parliament, is not Inconsistent with a Free Government* (1698).
Meanwhile *Mercurius Politicus* praised the *Argument* as a "smart Pamphlet".
Upon this, Toland issued a second part to his *State-Anatomy*, embroidering
upon Boyer's attack on Defoe, and the "Arguer" came back with *A Farther
Argument against Ennobling Foreigners* (**369**, *q.v.*), in which he dismissed the
idea that Defoe had any part in the affair.

This is one of the thorniest problems in Defoe attribution, the arguments
for Defoe's authorship of the two attacks on Toland and against it being
both very formidable. Much turns on the credibility or otherwise of the
denial of Defoe's authorship in *A Farther Argument*, and it must be admitted
that certain features of this have a dubious ring. (Defoe, we are told, "was
no more Author of this Book than the Man in the Moon: Nay, *as I hear*, for
I have no Knowledge of the Man, he has been sick in his Bed all the
while".) It would, moreover, not be impossible to imagine a scenario
according to which Defoe, in his enthusiasm to attack Toland, failed to
realise quite how fatally he was laying himself open to the charge of self-
contradiction. The extraordinary weakness of *A Farther Argument* as a
defence of Defoe (i.e. its casual assertion that even if, by hypothesis, Defoe
had been the author of the *Argument* and had contradicted himself, it would
not have been a matter of any importance) could thus be regarded as a
kind of embittered shrug of the shoulders.

We discussed the problem at length in the *Canonisation* (pp. 157–60) and,
after some further thought, we have come back to the view we expressed
there: that for the moment the complications and anomalies involved in
assigning these two pamphlets to Defoe seem too great, and it is safest to
regard his authorship as unproven.

360 An Account of the Swedish and Jacobite Plot

London: Printed for S. Popping, J. Harrison and A. Dodd, 1717

ATTRIBUTION: Moore; Novak (as "Probably by Defoe").

An extreme-Whig diatribe against the Jacobite-Swedish invasion-plot (the "Gyllenberg Affair") and the implicitly Jacobite tone of the report of recent events connected with it (the arrest of Baron Goertz, etc.) in the *Post-Boy* for 23 February. It represents Charles XII of Sweden as a savage and brutal tyrant and rebukes the Tory press for reflecting critically on George I's taking possession of Bremen and Verden.

The publisher of the *Post-Boy*, John Morphew (who was in fact arrested on 25 February for the issue mentioned above) was also the publisher of *Mercurius Politicus*, with which Defoe is known to have been associated. It thus seems unlikely that Defoe would have launched a violent attack on him. (He showed concern when Morphew was arrested again, in May of the following year, on account of a passage in *Mercurius Politicus* – see *Letters*, p. 456.) It would also be hard to imagine the same author writing this rancorous piece and *What if the Swedes Should Come?* (Moore, **364**), which appeared two or three weeks later and adopted an altogether different tone towards Charles XII.

362 An Expostulatory Letter, to the B[ishop] of B[angor]

London. Printed for E. Smith [1717]

ATTRIBUTION: Trent (*CHEL*); Hutchins, Moore, Novak.

An elegant polemic, attacking with polite sarcasm Bishop Hoadly's *Preservative against the Principles of the Non-Jurors* (1716) – a work written against the posthumous *Collection of Papers* of the Non-Juror George Hickes. It says that Hoadly, basking in the approval of the Whig Government, employs unfair weapons against the Non-Jurors, who are in too vulnerable a position to argue with him on equal terms; but, more importantly, he bases himself on a totally fallacious argument, i.e. that James II was deposed for being a Catholic (whereas he was deposed for being a tyrant). If Hoadly's thesis were correct, it would be a severe satire on the Bench of Bishops, who must have been greatly at fault either in crowning a king who was incapable of ruling, or in deposing him once they had done so. If Monmouth's rebellion had succeeded, what would have been said of those Protestants who came out against him and his supporters as traitors and rebels? Hoadly, in fact, by placing all the emphasis merely on James's religion, devalues the Revolution.

With this clever and effective pamphlet one is placed in a familiar difficulty. It would by no means be absurd to imagine that Defoe wrote it: it employs the sort of skilful needling that he was adept in, and nothing in it obviously conflicts with his known views. Yet we are not aware of any really compelling reason for connecting it with him (and Trent offers none).

365a Christianity No Creature of the State ... By the Author of The Case of the Protestant Dissenters Fairly Stated

[Dublin]: Re-printed in the Year 1717

ATTRIBUTION: Moore; Novak (as "Perhaps by Defoe").

Argues the folly of trying to make a "state engine" or "state creature" of the Church and scornfully denies that Christ ever designed a "Spiritual *Bridewell*" or a "Sin-Office". Asks why must the country be at the expense of a standing army, just because the Tories oppose the repeal of the laws against the Dissenters? Hopes that "some of our Senators" will remember their promises to the Dissenters, for this – if ever – is the time for them to be kept.

According to the *Monthly Catalogue* this tract was first published in London by J. Roberts in April 1717. Moore first attributed this Dublin reprint to Defoe in his article "Defoe Acquisitions at the Huntington Library", *HLQ*, 28 (1964), 45–57, saying that it "has obvious similarities to other Defoe tracts, such as *The Question Fairly Stated* (1717)", but that it is "more original than most of Defoe's writings on the subject". He notes that it "quotes Defoe's personal motto, 'Probitas laudatur & alget'".

On the evidence of the title-page, this attribution presumably stands or falls with that of **335** (*q.v.*) which we de-attribute. The passage from p. 20 which Moore quotes in his article, claiming that "at least half a dozen Defoe idioms occur within a space of only nine lines", does not actually ring quite right for Defoe.

366 The Danger and Consequence of Disobliging the Clergy

London: Printed for J. Baker, 1716–17

ATTRIBUTION: Crossley (a tentative attribution only); Trent (*Nation*, as "Most probably Defoe's"), Hutchins, Moore, Novak.

Published in April 1717, a letter in ranting style addressed to a Noble Lord in the country on the Gyllenberg Affair, the rumoured plan to reform the universities and the need for a drastic purge of High-Church clergy there and in the country generally. (This part is closely akin to *Reasons for a Royal Visitation* (**367**, *q.v.*), making similar use of Serjeant Miller's *Account of the University of Cambridge*.) The Dissenters are asserted to be, "one and all, Heart and Hand, Universally, and without Exception, to one Man, in the Interest of King *George*" (p. 21), and the King is encouraged to maintain a standing army for some time longer, even if no Swedish invasion takes place.

Mercurius Politicus, with which Defoe is known to have been associated, refers to this and **367** as "virulent pamphlets and libels" (April 1717, p. 234). The crude style of argument, unmitigated Whiggism and unqualified praise of the Dissenters make this unlikely to be by Defoe.

367 Reasons for a Royal Visitation

London: Printed for J. Roberts, 1717

ATTRIBUTION: Crossley; Trent (*Nation*), Hutchins, Moore, Novak (as "Probably by Defoe").

Published in April 1717, a furious Whiggish diatribe, written in the person of a member of the Church of England, against the scandalous character of a portion of the clergy (the Jacobite faction), which it blames on the degeneracy of the universities, these being in urgent need of a royal visitation and a severe purge. It quotes extensively from Serjeant Miller's *Account of the University of Cambridge*, which links the corruption of the clergy to the practice of enforcing vain oaths in the unversities. (The tract is prompted by the Coronation Day riots in Oxford in October 1716 and the Gyllenberg Plot.) The title-page carries a quotation from *The True-Born Englishman* ("Of all the plagues with which Mankind are curst, / Ecclesiastick Tyranny's the worst").

This ranting piece, consistently Church of England in its viewpoint and containing some abusive passing references to "Sectaries" and "Phanaticks", never suggests Defoe. *Mercurius Politicus* (see above, **366**) calls it and

366 "virulent pamphlets and libels", published in order to bring the universities "into an entire Subjection to their worst Enemies". It is possible that the quotation from *The True-Born Englishman* encouraged an attribution to Defoe, but if so with little reason. Pat Rogers notes in his "Addenda and Corrigenda: Moore's *Checklist* of Defoe", *PBSA*, 75 (1981), 60–64, that "Oldmixon is at least as strong a candidate".

369 A Farther Argument against Ennobling Foreigners

London: Printed for E. Moore, 1717

ATTRIBUTION: Boyer, in *Political State*, February 1717, pp. 142–43; Trent (*Nation*), Hutchins, Moore, Novak.

See note on **359**, above.

370 The Conduct of Robert Walpole, Esq.

London: Printed for T. Warner, 1717

ATTRIBUTION: Trent (*Nation*); Hutchins, Moore, Novak.

Published in May 1717, a panegyric of Walpole occasioned by his resignation from the Government on 10 April, in sympathy with his brother-in-law Townshend, who had been dismissed the previous day. The author quotes at length from *Fair Payment no Spunge* (Moore, **363**), noting that some have "said it was done by Daniel de Foe" (p. 59).

Trent offers little evidence, apart from his "tests", for attributing this windy and vacuous piece to Defoe and resorts to somewhat desperate speculations to explain why the tract is able to quote, as an epigraph, six lines of verse from a play by George Sewell, *The Tragedy of Sir Walter Raleigh*, which was not performed or printed until 1719. It is possible that this is the pamphlet that Boyer, in his list of attributions to Defoe, refers to as *A Letter to the Right Hon. Robert Walpole, Esq.*, but if any attribution is to be made, the more likely candidate would evidently be Sewell, who produced a further defence of Walpole (and Townshend), *The Resigners Vindicated*, the following year. See our article, "Defoe, Trent, and the 'Defection'", *RES*, n.s., 44 (1993), 70–76.

371 The Report Reported: or, The Weakness and Injustice of the Proceedings of the Convocation in their Censure of the L[or]d B[isho]p of Bangor, Examin'd and Expos'd

London: Printed for S. Baker, 1717

ATTRIBUTION: Trent (*CHEL*); Hutchins, Moore, Novak (as "Probably by Defoe").

Published in May 1717, it argues that Andrew Snape, in his attack on Hoadly in his *Letter to the Bp. of Bangor*, acted in a way unbecoming to a Christian minister and a gentleman, and that the *Report* (or "Representation") of the Lower House of Convocation, which has been published without authority, is "empty and trifling", as well as unjust in its accusations against Hoadly.

This is one of eight new "Bangorian" attributions to Defoe made by Trent, on internal evidence. There is evidence (see e.g. *A Declaration of Truth to Benjamin Hoadly* [1717], Moore, **379**) leading one to believe that Defoe took a detached and ironical attitude towards the Bangorian controversy, relishing the chance to tease both Hoadly's High-Church enemies and Hoadly himself, and to moralise about the disgracefulness of so much clerical mud-slinging – thereby dissociating himself from the Government's wholeheartedly pro-Hoadly line. This inclines us to reject the present uninspired and uncritical defence of Hoadly.

372 A Short View of the Conduct of the King of Sweden

London: Printed and Sold by A. Dodd [1717]

ATTRIBUTION: Trent (*CHEL*); Hutchins, Moore, Novak.

An ironical condensation and adaptation of *The History of the Wars of Charles XII* (1715) (**322**, *q.v.*), giving it a pretendedly pro-Jacobite slant.
See our note on **322**, and discussion in *Canonisation*, pp. 17–28.

373 A General Pardon Consider'd

London: Printed for S. Baker, 1717

ATTRIBUTION: Trent (*CHEL*); Hutchins, Moore, Novak (as "Probably by Defoe").

Dutiful reflections on the announcement in the speech from the throne on 6 May 1717 that the King contemplates a reduction in the armed forces and is preparing an Act of Grace. The author acknowledges that the King cannot pardon all offenders but cites historical examples of erstwhile rebels who later served their ruler loyally. He distinguishes with legal nicety between an Act of Grace, a General Pardon, an Act of Oblivion, an Act of Indemnity and a General Amnesty.

The bland and orotund style of this piece never suggests Defoe, and there seems no obvious reason for associating it with him.

374 Observations on the Bishop's Answer to Dr. Snape

London: Printed for S. Baker, 1717

ATTRIBUTION: Trent (*CHEL*); Hutchins, Moore, Novak.

Published in May 1717, a laborious critique of Hoadly's *Answer* to Andrew Snape's *Letter to the Bishop of Bangor*, saying that a good deal of the fault lies with Hoadly, for not making his meaning clear, and complaining of the "coarse" treatment given to Snape by Hoadly's supporters.

This extremely prosy piece, in our view, never for a moment suggests Defoe. (Cf. our note on **371**.)

375 A Vindication of Dr. Snape

London: Printed for A. Dodd [1717]

ATTRIBUTION: Trent (*CHEL*); Hutchins, Moore, Novak (as "Probably by Defoe").

A sensible but pedestrian statement of the position that, though there are things one can respect in Hoadly's doctrines, the venom of his supporters towards Andrew Snape is unjustified, and Snape has really had the best of the argument. Hoadly, preaching at a time when there is much talk of improving the legal position of the Dissenters, offers a bolder and more radical argument for this than they themselves or their propagandists have dared to put forward: i.e. the invalidity of *any* legal interference in matters of conscience and religion. But, having done so, with what logic can he remain a Church of England bishop? Moreover, Snape appears to be correct in claiming that the Apostles themselves believed they wielded authority in their own right.

The line of argument is similar to the one adopted, teasingly, in *A Declaration of Truth to Benjamin Hoadly* (Moore, **379**), which there is good reason to attribute to Defoe; and on p. 4 we find a quotation from Rochester ("Fellows who ne're were heard or read of, / If thou writ'st on, will write thy Head off"), which is also used in Defoe's *Fifth Essay at Removing National Prejudices* (Moore, **134**), as well as in *A Friendly Rebuke to*

One Parson Benjamin (Moore, **409**) which is probably by Defoe. On the other hand, one never seems to hear Defoe's voice in this tract. There is hardly a trace of wit or polemical verve. Note, for instance, the excessively "sober-sided" remarks about Hoadly's sermon having been "*unseasonable*" (p. 5). This inclines one to say that, since the only piece of evidence pointing towards Defoe that Trent manages to bring is the Rochester quotation, the case for an attribution has not really been made.

It may be noted that this seems to be earlier than Moore, **374** (see above), for it speaks as though Hoadly had not yet published his *Answer* to Snape, to which **374** is a rejoinder.

376 A Reply to the Remarks upon the Lord Bishop of Bangor's Treatment of the Clergy and Convocation. Said to be Written by Dr. Sherlock

London: Printed for S. Baker, 1717

ATTRIBUTION: Trent (*CHEL*); Hutchins, Moore, Novak.

A pugnacious pro-Hoadly piece, saying that it is surprising that Thomas Sherlock (the leading drafter of Convocation's Report) should have undertaken the same "dirty" task as Andrew Snape has already been so severely chastised for. Sherlock even has the temerity to hint that the King and Government are hostile to the Church, and to threaten Hoadly with future retribution, though five years ago Sherlock was expressing much the same views as Hoadly.

One can no discern no obvious grounds for associating this with Defoe. (Cf. our note on **371**.)

380 A History of the Clemency of our English Monarchs

London: Printed for N. Mist and Sold by T. Warner, 1717

ATTRIBUTION: Trent (Bibliography); Moore, Novak (as "Probably by Defoe").

Published in September 1717, a reply, though not declaredly so, to a pamphlet of the same title by the Non-Juror Matthias Earbery, which censured the harsh treatment of the rebels captured at Preston in 1716 and was condemned as treasonable. The present tract claims on p. 24 that George I, by pardoning some rebels who showed no sign of repentance, showed a mercy that "extended even beyond that of God himself".

Excerpts from this tract were printed in *Mercurius Politicus* for September

1717, side by side with some from Earbery's, Boyer having already printed the latter excerpts in the *Political State* for August. *Mercurius Politicus* passes no judgement on the present tract, except to comment that "seeing the Whig Author, as he calls himself [i.e. Boyer], *though in this he seems to be doing the Work of the Tories*, has published the Tory book, we think we must let the Tory Author publish the Whig book".

The absurdly eulogistic tone towards the King and (pp. 9–10) towards Charles I and Charles II, and an imputation on p. 21 that the defeated Tory ministers began to plan an armed rebellion on the first day of the King's arrival on English soil, would come improbably from Defoe, nor does the measured Ciceronian sentence construction suggest him. The fact that excerpts were published in *Mercurius Politicus* hardly in itself constitutes evidence for Defoe's authorship.

383 A Letter to Andrew Snape ... By the Author of *The Declaration of Truth*

London: Printed for T. Warner, 1717

ATTRIBUTION: Crossley; Trent (*Nation*), Hutchins, Moore, Novak.

Published in August 1717, a "Quaker" rebuke to Andrew Snape for the uncharitableness of his *Second Letter* to Hoadly, whose Christian meekness in his replies puts him to shame.

The line taken in this is so different from that in *A Declaration of Truth to Benjamin Hoadly* (1717), which seems certainly to be by Defoe, and *A Friendly Rebuke to One Parson Benjamin* (1719), which appears very probably so, that we are inclined to question its claim to be by the author of the former. Having teased Hoadly so cleverly in *A Declaration of Truth*, praising him for his "Quaker" outlook and saying it will plainly not be long before he gives up his bishopric, it seems unlikely that Defoe would soon afterwards have given Hoadly such simple and unreserved commendation – i.e. commendation with no "catch" in it.

It is worth noting that among the pamphlets listed in the bibliography of the Bangorian controversy included in the *Works of Benjamin Hoadly* (1773) is one entitled *The Quaker's Declaration of Truth to Benjamin Hoadly, Called Bishop of Bangor* (T. Warner, 25 June, 1717) (ii, 400). We have so far been unable to locate a copy.

384 The Case of the War in Italy Stated

London: Printed for T. Warner, 1718 [for 1717]

ATTRIBUTION: Lee; Trent (*CHEL*), Hutchins, Moore, Novak.

A bellicose pamphlet (in fact published in December 1717) arguing that it may be necessary for the King to intervene against Spain, whose aggression against the Emperor is both a threat to the balance of power in Europe and a personal insult to the King, who has been attempting mediation. The "harangues" of the peace party in Britain, alleging the nation's exhaustion and impoverishment and the bad effect a war might have on Britain's trade with Spain, have a certain superficial plausibility, but to abandon the Emperor now would be to give away all that the late war was fought for.

The tract argues an almost exactly opposite position to the "Sir Andrew Politick" letters beginning in February 1718 in *Mist's Journal*, which external evidence strongly suggests were written by Defoe (see our article "Defoe and 'Sir Andrew Politick'", *British Journal for Eighteenth-Century Studies*, 17 [1994], 27–39). This contradiction, and the fact that in known writings like the *Review* Defoe always seems careful not to figure as a war-monger, argue against his authorship.

385 The Annals of King George, Year the Third

London: Printed for A. Bell, T. Vernon, J. Osbourn and W. Taylor, 1718 [for 1717]

ATTRIBUTION: Moore.

See note on 351.

386 Considerations on the Present State of Affairs

London: Printed for J. Roberts, 1718

ATTRIBUTION: Trent (*CHEL*); Hutchins, Moore, Novak.

A blanket defence of the King (and by implication the Stanhope-Sunderland administration) against his unnamed enemies and critics, framed as a commentary on his speech at the opening of a new parliamentary session on 21 November 1717. It asserts the extreme danger of faction in the present alarming juncture in European affairs (the renewal of hostilities between Spain and the Emperor), and hence the need for a Protestant League.

The style of this platitudinous and sermonising tract never suggests Defoe, nor does the Latitudinarian stance adopted on p. 22, which seems to imply that it is almost a matter of indifference whether one is a Dissenter or a Churchman. (Defoe, by contrast, frequently argues that a conscientious Dissenter ought to sacrifice all his worldly hopes rather than be false to his beliefs.)

387 The Defection Farther Consider'd

London: Printed and Sold by William Boreham, 1718

ATTRIBUTION: Trent (*Nation*); Hutchins, Moore, Novak.

This presents itself as the "Second Part" of a famous anonymous attack on Walpole and Townshend, *The Defection Consider'd* (1717), by the deist Matthew Tindal. It argues that the only name for the defecting Whigs (Walpole in particular) is not "resigners" but "deserters". Their action proves that they were hypocrites, concerned solely with their own self-interest, all along; and their "unmanly" insinuations against the King himself are practically treasonable (p. 13). It thus takes a diametrically opposite stance to a pamphlet entitled *Some Persons Vindicated against the Author of the Defection*, published a fortnight later (28 January 1718), which Trent also ascribed to Defoe (an attribution supported by a piece of external evidence). His basis for ascribing the present pamphlet is, as usual, stylistic "tests", combined with the belief that Defoe could positively be expected to confute himself – evidently in itself no reason at all for supposing that, in a given case, he did so.

See further our article, "Defoe, Trent, and the 'Defection'", *RES*, n.s., 44 (1993), 70–76.

388 Some Persons Vindicated against the Author of *The Defection*

London: Printed for William Boreham, 1718

ATTRIBUTION: Trent (*Nation*); Hutchins, Moore, Novak.

Published 28 January 1718, a furious, but empty and generalising, reply to Tindal's *The Defection Consider'd* of December 1717, in which Tindal blamed Walpole and Townshend for "defecting", for cynical motives, thereby creating a serious division in the Whig party. The present tract argues that Tindal's reflections on the motives of Walpole and Townshend are a gross injustice to men of unblemished patriotism, and that to claim, as Tindal does, that their "defection" has put the whole country at risk is to insult the competence of the present administration.

In *Memoirs of the Life and Writings of Matthew Tindal*, published by Curll in 1733, p. 57, this is said to have been "Written by Daniel De Foe". It is, however, difficult to credit that Defoe, who there is reason to believe took a detached and ironic attitude towards the "defection" affair, could have written such an incompetent and partisan piece. Since the dedicatory epistle to the *Memoirs* of Tindal is signed "E.C.", it may be that the attribution to Defoe is the work of Edmund Curll, several of whose posthumous ascriptions to Defoe strike us as distinctly questionable.

389 Memoirs of the Life and Eminent Conduct of ... Daniel Williams

London: Printed for E. Curll, 1718

ATTRIBUTION: Wilson ("It has occurred to the present writer, whether De Foe was not the author"); Lee, Trent (*CHEL*), Hutchins, Moore, Novak.

A memoir of the famous Presbyterian divine Daniel Williams (1643?–1716), who served the congregation at Hand Alley in Bishopsgate Street for twenty-seven years, advised William III on Irish affairs, and by his will left large trust-funds for the training of English dissenting clergy in Scotland and the collection which formed the nucleus of the present Dr. Williams' Library in Bloomsbury.

A re-issue of this work was advertised by Curll, after Defoe's death, as "Written by Daniel De Foe" in a list of twenty-three "Lives of Eminent Persons, Printed Only for E. Curll", included at the end of the 4th edition of William Pittis's *Dr. Radcliffe's Life and Letters* (1736). A further possible connection with Defoe is that it reprints without acknowledgement a passage from his *The Parallel* (1705).

The Curll attribution is obviously a strong piece of external evidence. Nevertheless, the ascription is very hard to credit, in the first place because the author writes that "perhaps no single Person remains alive, that has had so general and so long a knowledge of, and so particular an intimacy with the Doctor's Conduct in the Things here spoken of, or so many Opportunities to be acquainted with the particulars, as the Person who has handed these Memoirs to the Publick" – whereas we can call to mind no reference whatever to Williams in Defoe's letters or other writings, and certainly nothing to suggest that the two were intimate. Secondly, the work is described on the title-page as "Address'd to Mr. Peirce". James

Peirce of Exeter was at this moment the centre of a violent schism among the Dissenters, being the leader of the party accused of Arianism, and it is hard to imagine Defoe, who always came down very severely on Socinianism and Arianism, making such a dedication, even for purposes of disguise. (*Mercurius Politicus*, with which he was associated, was censorious in its issues for April and May 1719 about the "ill-natur'd Quarrel" in the Dissenting body and makes it plain that it thinks Peirce an Arian and a prevaricator.) Thirdly, the author (p. 26 – mis-numbered) is more indulgent towards Occasional Conformity than fits with Defoe's implacable opposition to it. Fourthly, the clumsiness and parsonical tone of the prose do not suggest him. (Everything would seem to suggest that the author was one of Williams' clerical friends, of the Peircite faction.)

That the rascally Curll might have ascribed the work to Defoe when he was safely dead, as a sales device, seems a serious possibility, since Defoe is generally credited with a ferocious attack on "Curlicism" in *Mist's Journal* for 5 April 1718, and certainly speaks bitterly of Curll in a letter to De la Faye on 4 June 1718, so that it seems unlikely he would have employed him as a publisher. We agree with Rodney Baine that the other work published by Curll included in Moore's *Checklist*, i.e. *The History of… Mr. Duncan Campbell* (**432**, *q.v.*), is unlikely to be by Defoe.

390 Mr. De La Pillonniere's Vindication … By the Author of *The Lay-man's Vindication*

London: Printed for T. Warner, 1718

ATTRIBUTION: Trent (*CHEL*); Hutchins, Moore, Novak.

A prosy and heavy-handed piece, accusing Andrew Snape of false reasoning in his *Second Letter* to Hoadly (of 28 June 1717): for even if Snape succeeded in blackening Hoadly's private character, this would have no bearing on his views. It also ridicules Snape's theory that Hoadly's protege Pillonniere is still a covert Jesuit, and praises Hoadly's own conduct in his controversy with Snape. (Its date is roughly indicated by the fact that it refers to Pillonniere's own *Answer to Dr. Snape's Accusation* of the end of October 1717 and Snape's *Vindication of a Passage in Dr. Snape's Second Letter*, also of late October.)

Trent offers nothing in the way of positive evidence to support this attribution, relying merely on "characteristic touches" suggesting Defoe. The main point to consider is the title-page claim that the tract is by "the Author of the Lay-man's Vindication". About a year earlier, a powerful attack on the non-juror Laurence Howell was published under the title *The Layman's Vindication of the Church of England*. As Trent was the first to point out, there is a good deal of internal evidence suggesting Defoe as the author of this, and he takes it to be the work referred to on the title-page of *Mr. De La Pillonniere's Vindication*. The two works are so utterly unlike each other, however, that it is difficult to see them as by the same writer. The only other candidate, *The Lay-Man's Vindication of the Convocation's Charge against the Bishop of Bangor* (1717), by Edward Hart, must be ruled out on grounds of content, it having been written in support of Snape and against Hoadly.

391 A Brief Answer to a Long Libel

London: Printed and Sold by William Boreham, 1718

ATTRIBUTION: Moore; Novak (as "Perhaps by Defoe").

Published 13 February, a robust but not otherwise remarkable reply to *The Danger of the Church's Establishment* by the High-Church writer and cleric Thomas Lewis, author of the periodical *The Scourge*. Lewis collected quotations from Dissenting authors, to demonstrate their dangerousness to the established Church. The present pamphlet replies that for the most part the quotations do not attack the Church itself but "High Flying raging Party-men" and other "immoral, scandalous" clergy in it, and moreover the works he cites are probably not all by Dissenters.

Though nothing in the tract would rule Defoe out as the author, there does not seem to be evidence warranting a positive ascription.

392 A Letter from the Jesuits to Father De La Pillonniere: In Answer to the Letter Sent to Them by that Father, and Published by Dr. Snape, in his *Vindication*

London: Printed for T. Warner, 1718

ATTRIBUTION: Moore; Novak.

In late 1717 Andrew Snape produced a *Vindication of a Passage in Dr. Snape's Second Letter to the Bishop of Bangor*, and at the end of this he placed an imaginary letter from Pillonniere to his Jesuit superiors, explaining his schemes. The present tract, published in February 1718, is presumably prompted by that fictitious letter. It takes the form of a pretended rebuke to La Pillonniere from the Jesuits for his clumsy handling of his popish mission in England. It is naive of him, they say, to think he can over-reach Hoadly, "the *Greatest* and *Ablest*, Enemy that we ever had in England" (p. 13). Further, they say, he will get nowhere by speaking up for free thought and preaching mutual tolerance and unity among Protestants: indeed they fear he is in danger of actually going over to Hoadly's party. All the same, they comfort themselves, his association with Hoadly has very satisfactorily provoked intolerance from Hoadly's enemies (p. 24).

A passage on p. 39 offers strong evidence that this is not by Defoe, i.e. the one in which the Jesuits blame Pillonniere greatly for translating the works of *Clarke*, whom he ought to be reviling as "A *Socinian*, a *Deist*, and an *Atheist*". The implication, for the reader, that this is a praiseworthy token of Pillonniere's broadminded and tolerant outlook is most unlikely to come from Defoe, who was himself habitually intolerant of free-thinkers of the Clarke, Toland, Whiston school.

393 A Golden Mine of Treasure Open'd for the Dutch

London: Printed in the Year 1718

ATTRIBUTION: Moore (as "Probably, not certainly, by Defoe", and in the Second Supplement as "Certainly by Defoe"); Novak (as "Probably by Defoe").

This tract falls into two parts, the first thirty-two pages being supposedly by a foreigner and the succeeding "Application" by an Englishman. The title-page date "1718" is somewhat puzzling, since the tract deals with the Gyllenberg Affair of early 1717 (the arrest of the Swedish ambassador on 29 January 1717 and seizure of his papers, as evidence of a threatened Swedish-supported Jacobite invasion). It is a highly inflammatory and seditious high Tory attack on the Whig government for exploiting and exaggerating the imaginary threat of a Swedish invasion and for violating the rights of an ambassador, as a pretext for furthering George I's designs on the duchies of Bremen and Verden and "the private Views" of the House of Hanover, "who are Strangers, and even in many things Opposites in Interest to the *English*" (p. 22).

This reckless Jacobite production strikes one as a most implausible attribution.

394 Miserere Cleri ... Being a Short View of the Pernicious Consequences of the Clergy's Intermedling with Affairs of State

London: Printed for W. Boreham [1718]

ATTRIBUTION: Moore; Novak.

This is, in fact, as the title indicates, merely a re-issue of item **287** (*q.v.*), and on p. 34 it refers anachronistically to "the late *Riot and Murder at Bristol*", though adding "and the Tumults and Rebellion since that". On p. 9 a reference is added to "a certain Clergyman" who has "embroild this whole unhappy Nation". One wonders whether, despite the fact that **287** was thoroughly Whiggish, this addition is not intended as a hit at Hoadly and the Bangorian controversy. There are other minor changes, but this is the most substantial.

No reason suggests itself for believing Defoe to be connected with this re-issue, any more than with the original pamphlet.

395 Some Reasons why it could not be Expected the Government wou'd Permit the Speech ... of James Shepheard ... to be Printed

London: Printed for W. Boreham, 1718

ATTRIBUTION: Trent (Bibliography); Moore, Novak (as "Probably by Defoe").

A blustering and bombastic pulpit-style reprobation of the "execrable Assassine and Murtherer" James Shepheard, the "Coach-maker's boy", who planned to murder George I. It says that the Government no doubt had two good reasons for not publishing Shepheard's "Dying Speech": (1) that it was too horrible and blasphemous; (2) that it was almost certainly not written by him but by the wily Jesuits who perverted him. The letter, says the author, was full of internal contradictions but clearly designed to exculpate the Pretender.

The tract was highly praised and summarised at some length in *Mercurius Britannicus* for March 1718, with the comment that "It is reported, that this Piece has been Published by Order or Direction of some Persons too high to name, and that the Government itself has thought it highly necessary to have the Eyes of the abused People opened in a thing of such Consequence; but this I do not assert" (p. 107).

It is difficult to see why Moore or Trent should have attributed this to Defoe. The fact of its having been summarised in *Mercurius Britannicus* suggests nothing in particular about its authorship, and the tone never remotely suggests Defoe. (It may be noted further that whereas the Whiggish *Mercurius Britannicus* comes down harshly on Shepheard, *Mercurius Politicus*, which also reported the case in March 1718, takes a more compassionate line.)

*396 The Jacobites Detected

London: Printed for J. Roberts, 1718

ATTRIBUTION: Trent (Bibliography); Moore (as "Very probably, not certainly, by Defoe"), Novak (as "Perhaps by Defoe").

A furious piece of railing against the wiles of Jacobites and their skill in perverting young minds – prompted by the trial of James Shepheard for plotting to assassinate George I. Gives an implausible description of a Jacobite oath-taking ceremony and delivers a slashing attack on *Mist's Journal* (pp. 27–28). It says that the Jacobites should be given the same medicine as a Bishop wished to see inflicted on the Dissenters at the time of the Schism Bill, i.e. to be rooted out from our *'Canaan'*. The author claims to be young and inexperienced, indeed "*infra aetatem*" (p. 30).

This crude and foolish piece seems a most unconvincing attribution.

397 Dr. Sherlock's Vindication of the Test Act Examin'd, and the False Foundations of it Exposed: In Answer to so much of his Book against the Bishop of Bangor, as Relates to the Protestant Dissenters

London: Printed for S. Popping, J. Harrison and A. Dodd, 1718

ATTRIBUTION: Moore; Novak (as "Perhaps by Defoe").

A sober tract, answering Thomas Sherlock's famous *Vindication of the Corporation and Test Acts* (1718), which goes back to the first passing of the Test Act to show that it was not originally designed for use against the Dissenters but the Papists, though later it came to be so used. Sherlock's argument that Anglican communion is the *foundation* not the *effect* of the Act is fallacious: the Act undoubtedly *is* a Test of what was not subject to a Test before (pp. 38–39). Further, it encourages giving the sacrament to atheists and heathens.

The only argument hitherto put forward for attributing this to Defoe is that on pp. 9–12 it refers to and quotes (in inverted commas) a couple of pages from "a small Tract written some Time since by an unknown

Author, and call'd, *The Question Fairly Stated*, &c.", a tract also attributed to Defoe (Moore, **365**). This does not in itself seem a compelling argument for assigning the present work to Defoe, and the style does not greatly suggest him, nor does the kindly reference to Occasional Conformity on p. 36.

398 A Brief Comment upon His Majesty's Speech: Being Reasons for Strengthening the Church of England by Taking off the Penal Laws against Dissenters. By One Called a Low-Church-Man

London: Printed for T. Warner, 1718

ATTRIBUTION: Crossley; Trent (*Nation*; as "Very probably Defoe's"), Hutchins, Moore, Novak (as "Perhaps by Defoe").

A discussion of the King's speech of 21 November 1717, which urged a "strengthening of the Protestant Interest", interpreting this as a promise to remove the penal disabilities of the Dissenters. Notes that "while these Sheets were in the Press", news came of the "unhappy breach or misunderstanding" at Court (i.e. the King's quarrel with the Prince of Wales). Are not those who gloat over this, it asks, the same people as want to perpetuate the divisions between Churchmen and Dissenters?

A well-written tract, repeating many of the standard arguments in favour of the Dissenters, with some neat and inventive turns of phrase. The *persona* of a "Low-Church Man" is only occasionally in evidence. It would be quite possible to imagine Defoe as the author, the phrasing in places being suggestive of him, but there is nothing really striking in the way of internal evidence to point to him.

399 A Vindication of the Press

London: Printed for T. Warner, 1718

ATTRIBUTION: Trent (*CHEL*); Hutchins, Moore, Novak.

Conventional reflections on the benefits of a free press, the harmfulness of much contemporary criticism and the qualities of good writing, by (as he describes himself) a "young Author", a devout Churchman and despiser of conventicles, and an enthusiastic devotee of the contemporary theatre.

In our article "*A Vindication of the Press* (1718): Not by Defoe?", *PBSA*, 78 (1984), 355–60, we argued for the implausibility of this Trent attribution. See also a defence of the attribution by Maximillian Novak, "*A Vindication of the Press* and the Defoe Canon", *Studies in English Literature*

1500–1900, 27 (1987), 399–411; our reply, "The Defoe Canon Again", *PBSA*, 82 (1988), 95–98; and a further discussion by Laura A. Curtis, "The Attribution of *A Vindication of the Press* to Daniel Defoe", *Studies in Eighteenth-Century Culture*, 18 (1988), 433–44.

400 A Letter from Some Protestant Dissenting Laymen

London: Printed and Sold by W. Graves, 1718

ATTRIBUTION: Moore; Novak (as "Probably by Defoe").

Published in May 1718, a complaint, in the form of a letter from some "Protestant Dissenting Laymen", that nothing was done to relieve the Dissenters in the last session of Parliament. This, it says, was no doubt because of the unprincipled behaviour of the Whig "defectors" (i.e. the Walpole/Townshend faction), but the loyal and peace-loving conduct of the Dissenters over the past half-century deserved better of the nation.

On p. 18 there is a defence of Occasional Conformity against the strictures of "the most rigid of our Party". Since Defoe, as many of his known writings show, was one of this "most rigid" group, the attribution of this tract to him is implausible. Nothing in its prose style, moreover, suggests him.

401 Memoirs of Publick Transactions in the Life and Ministry of ... the D[uke] of Shrewsbury

London: Printed for Tho. Warner, 1718

ATTRIBUTION: Lee; Trent (*CHEL*), Hutchins, Moore, Novak.

A circumstantial and eulogistic account of the career of the Duke of Shrewsbury (who died 1 February 1718), depicting him as a man of honour and subtlety, whose apparent indolence was often a cunning device for avoiding factional quarrels. The author claims not to have been a close friend of his but to have been intimately involved in the public affairs he was concerned with. He cites (pp. 61–62) an informant who was a closer friend.

The tract discusses the authorship of *An Essay upon Publick Credit* (1710) (Moore, **187**, a work which there is strong evidence to prove was by Defoe; see *Letters*, pp. 276–77), saying it is sometimes attributed to Harley but could conceivably have been by Shrewsbury. It quotes passages from *The Minutes of Mnsr. Mesnager* (1717) (Moore, **377**) and from *Some Account of the Two Nights Court at Greenwich* (1716) (**334**, *q.v.*), and it refers to *Secret*

Memoirs of a Treasonable Conference at Somerset House (1717) (Moore, **354**), saying that if any such conference actually took place it does not show Shrewsbury in a bad light.

It is hard to make sense of certain details in this tract, and especially the discussion of *An Essay upon Publick Credit,* on the assumption that it is by Defoe. Lee does not explain why he attributed it to him, and possibly he was merely influenced by the various quotations from and references to works by, or ascribed to, Defoe.

402 A Letter from Paris, Giving an Account of the Death of the Late Queen Dowager

London: Printed and Sold by William Boreham, 1718

ATTRIBUTION: Trent (Bibliography); Moore, Novak (as "Probably by Defoe").

A supposed letter from the court of St. Germains, saying that the Queen Dowager, on her death-bed, confessed that the Pretender was not really her son, though the clergy have succeeded in hushing the matter up, putting it about that her reason for disowning the Pretender was that they had recently quarrelled. Contains some mild irony about the "liberty" that the British are reputed to give their tongues, as compared with France, where there are such effective methods of suppressing awkward rumours and opinions. The "Letter" is followed by "Observations" by the supposed recipient, saying that this revelation ought to spell the end of Jacobitism.

The "Letter" itself was reprinted in *Mercurius Britannicus* in May 1718, and this was probably the main reason why Trent (who believed that Defoe was conducting this Whiggish journal as well as the Tory *Mercurius Politicus*) attributed it to him. If so, it is hardly a very solid reason.

404 A History of the Last Session of the Present Parliament

London: Printed and Sold by W. Boreham, 1718

ATTRIBUTION: Trent (*CHEL*); Hutchins, Moore, Novak.

A detailed chronicle of the proceedings of Parliament during the session from October 1717 to March 1718. It is written from a broadly pro-Government standpoint, though it is not especially partisan in tone and gives Opposition speeches at length. The Introduction contains a blistering attack on Abel Boyer, and on pp. 76–77 it attempts to get him into trouble for suggesting, in the *Political State*, that the ministry was playing an unscrupulous trick over the Malt Bill. It says that Boyer's remarks were "such a Reflection upon His Majesty as I never met with in all this Reign".

The fact, seized on by Trent in his Bibliography, that the author (assuming the work to have a single compiler) is violently hostile to Boyer, certainly raises the possibility that it is by Defoe, since the two were long-standing enemies. Further, there is on p. 8 what looks like a borrowing from *Mercurius Politicus* (November 1717, p. 776), and Defoe is known to have been associated with that journal; but nothing much can be inferred from this, since the present work is evidently a compilation anyway. All in all, one is forced to regard this attribution as unproven.

405 A Letter to the Author of the *Flying-Post*

London: Printed for and Sold by A. Moore, 1718

ATTRIBUTION: Moore; Novak.

Published 11 October, a diatribe against George Ridpath for printing two anti-Jacobite items in his Whiggish *Flying-Post*, one of them reporting how some Edinburgh Jacobites had been struck by lightning while drinking confusion to King George, and the other in the form of a letter to the Bailiff of Brecon, addressed from the Grecian coffee-house, relating an attack by a Jacobite mob on the house of a Presbyterian minister in Brecon. The *Letter* follows on from two letters on similar lines recently published in the Tory and High-Church *Mist's Journal*, which had a long-standing political feud with the *Flying-Post*.

Defoe is known to have been associated with *Mist's Journal* at this time, and he was a personal enemy of Ridpath; but the sheer imbecility of this piece of facetious railing makes it impossible to imagine it as by him. See our *Canonisation*, pp. 162–64.

407 The History of the Reign of King George

London: Printed for N. Mist, 1719 [for 1718]

ATTRIBUTION: Crossley; Trent (*Nation*), Hutchins, Moore, Novak.

A very bulky chronicle of the first four years of the reign of George I. It is Tory in tone, anodyne in its references to the Pretender, eulogises Harley as "that noble Person" and draws attention to the pitiable condition of the Jacobite prisoners when at last released. It, however, includes lengthy extracts, sometimes, though more often not, in quotation marks, from the Whiggish *Annals of King George, Year the Second* and *Year the Third* (**351** and **385**, *qq.v.*). The author or compiler says (p. 203) "I have given these Accounts from the most certain Narrations of them which were made publick at that time, even by the Whiggs themselves, and even in their very Words".

Trent argues in the *Nation* for 11 July 1907 that the work is "indisputably Defoe's" and that it is "specially interesting because in it he maintains firmly, long after the extent of his exaggeration was ascertained, the truth of his extraordinary and well-known account of the blowing up of the island of St. Vincent" (see the single paragraph devoted to this on p. 229). The "well-known" account to which Trent refers first appeared in *Mist's Journal* on 5 July 1718, and was repudiated as untrue in the same *Journal* a month later. There is little here to support an attribution of the *History* to Defoe, and no serious case for the attribution has yet been made. Moore evidently regarded the relationship between this work and the *Annals* as an instance of Defoe writing for both camps. But the fact that the author draws attention to his borrowings from the *Annals* might, if anything, be thought to argue against his being their author. Moreover, Moore's case for attributing the *Annals* to Defoe is not convincing. See also our note on **351**, above.

408 The Memoirs of Majr. Alexander Ramkins

London: Printed for R. King and W. Boreham, 1719 [for 1718]

ATTRIBUTION: Arthur W. Secord (in an unpublished paper given to the Modern Language Association in 1929); Hutchins, Moore, Novak.

An account by a Highland major, now a prisoner in Avignon, of his experiences as a Jacobite serving officer, ending with a declaration of his change of heart and his present determination to support the Protestant succession.

The only extended discussion of the attribution of the *Memoirs* is by Beth S. Neman, in her informative unpublished Ph.D. thesis " *The Memoirs of Major Alexander Ramkins* by Daniel Defoe: A Scholarly Edition" (Miami University, 1976). As she points out, a Jacobite pamphlet of 1712 entitled *Mémoires du Chevalier de St. George* (Cologne) was attributed to a certain Alexander Rankine by Alice Shields and Andrew Lang in their biography of the Pretender, *The King Over the Water* (1907), but nothing can be found out about this Rankine, and whether there was a real-life Ramkins remains an open question. As there are no external grounds for associating the *Memoirs* with Defoe, Neman's case rests merely upon internal evidence of style and compatibility with other works by or attributed to him, and in our view it is not really strong enough to warrant a "probable" attribution.

410 Observations and Remarks upon the Declaration of War

London: Printed for W. Boreham, 1719

ATTRIBUTION: Moore; Novak (as "Probably by Defoe").

A dullish commentary (with lengthy quotations) on the French Regent's recent declaration of war on Spain and its accompanying manifesto. It describes the Regent's policies as reasonable and sincere (not a Machiavellian deception, as the Jacobites were alleging at one point), and it says that certain of his admissions about past events prove once and for all the folly of the Tory peace negotiations of 1711–12. It ridicules Cardinal Alberoni, as resembling a Fifth Monarchy Man who will have to have King Jesus on his side if Spain is to win.

   Moore gives no clue as to why he attributes this to Defoe, and it may be noted that the mockery of Spain conflicts with the outlook in the "Sir Andrew Politick" letters in *Mist's Journal*, for which there is evidence for thinking Defoe responsible (see the article cited in our note on **384**).

411 Merry Andrew's Epistle to his Old Master Benjamin ... Pestifero vomuit Colubar Sermonae Britannus. Prosp. de vit. Pelag.

London: Printed for E. Smith, 1719

ATTRIBUTION: Moore; Novak (as "Perhaps by Defoe").

A heavily facetious "parallel" in which a Merry Andrew twits his old master Benjamin (Hoadly), who, having defected from the College of Physicians (i.e. the Church), has set up his stage as a mountebank on Bangor bridge (Bangor was the home of Pelagius, a fact alluded to in the title) and has begun to behave more like a Quack (i.e. Dissenter) than a physician. The tract is aiming at Hoadly's contribution to the debate on the Bill to repeal the Occasional Conformity and Schism Acts, and possibly also to the Salters' Hall controversy.

   Mercurius Politicus reprinted lengthy excerpts in its issue for March 1719 (pp. 160–71), calling it an "unhappy Allegory" but "wrapt up in none of the worst Language". It refused to guess who the author might be. This is hardly grounds in itself for ascribing it to Defoe, and the wearisomely noisy facetiousness of the style does not really suggest him.

413 A Letter to the Dissenters

London: Printed for J. Roberts, 1719

ATTRIBUTION: Wilson; Lee, Trent (*CHEL*), Hutchins (who wrongly identifies it with the similarly-titled *Letter* of 1713), Moore, Novak.

An appeal to the Dissenters, in disarray after the acrimonious Salters' Hall conference, to behave in a less factious manner, for the sake of their own good name and in gratitude for the King's recent gracious remarks about them.

Wilson gives no reason for his attribution, and one wonders whether the fact that Defoe wrote an earlier tract of the same title may not have influenced him. One or two things seem a little to point away from Defoe. The earnest and pleading tone is in contrast to his usual tough and censorious one towards his fellow-Dissenters; and the complimentary reference to Thomas Bradbury and his *Answer to Some Reproaches Cast on those Dissenting Divines who Subscribed* (p. 4) would be surprising from the author of the satirical *A Friendly Epistle ... to Thomas Bradbury* (1715) (Moore, **305**).

415 Some Account of the Life ... of George Henry Baron De Goertz

London: Printed for T. Bickerton, 1719

ATTRIBUTION: Lee; Trent (*CHEL*), Hutchins, Moore, Novak.

Tells the story of Charles XII of Sweden's favourite minister, Baron de Goertz, mainly from the time of his arrest in Holland in 1717 during the Gyllenberg scandal. It relates how he eventually secured his release and got to Russia, where he managed to poison the Czar's mind against his allies (the Danes, the Princes of the Empire and the Poles) and to secure a *rapprochement* with Sweden; also how he was arrested on the sudden death of Charles XII in December 1718, on grounds of having "*put the King upon Dangerous Enterprizes*", and was executed in the following March. A seemingly well-informed tract, adulatory of Goertz and his master Charles and non-committal about the Gyllenberg affair.

Lee's explanation of his attribution (i, 301) is a revealing example of his over-confident and speculative methods. He takes it for granted that a report of Goertz's execution in *Mist's Journal* for 21 March 1719 is by Defoe and proceeds to imagine that Defoe, "being pressed for time and space ... probably took home the papers from Mist's office, to wait for a more favourable opportunity. Thus enabling me, after the lapse of a century and half, to prefix the above [the article in *Mist's Journal*] as his own preface, to an interesting pamphlet he shortly afterward published [i.e. the present work]". In fact, the authorship of the article in *Mist's Journal* does not have any obvious bearing on that of the present work, as the two do not present any close verbal parallels; and Lee's conjectures about Defoe taking some papers home from Mist's office are entirely gratuitous.

There seems no good reason for associating the tract with Defoe, and the adulation of Goertz, who was the principal organiser of the projected Jacobite invasion in 1717, would come oddly from him.

418 The Gamester

London: Printed for J. Roberts, 1719

ATTRIBUTION: Moore.

A hostile critique of a proposal by the New Company (or Society for Insurance of Ships) operating from Mercers' Hall, according to which they would insure the "Adventurers", who had bought up large quantities of tickets in the Government lotteries and were in danger of having them left on their hands, against loss. The tract and its successor **419**, attempt to show, according to the mathematical laws of probability, that the proposal is a cheat.

Moore ascribes this and **419** to Defoe on the strength of the fact that the former was warmly recommended in *Mercurius Politicus* for September 1719 (p. 554 *et seq.*). James Sutherland, in reviewing Moore's *Checklist* (*The Library*, 5th series, 17 [1963], 323–25) said – rightly, in our view – that this was to strain his theory that Defoe liked to recommend his own works "to breaking point".

419 The Gamester: No. II

London: Printed for J. Roberts, 1719

ATTRIBUTION: Moore.

See **418**.

421 Charity Still a Christian Virtue

London: Printed for T. Bickerton, 1719

ATTRIBUTION: Lee; Hutchins, Moore, Novak.

A lengthy and indignant account by a High Churchman of how a charity sermon, delivered by William Hendley at Chislehurst on behalf of a London charity school, was interrupted by two Whiggish local justices of the peace, who accused Hendley of begging for the Pretender, and how Hendley and the incumbent were subsequently tried at Rochester assizes and fined under the Vagrancy Act.

Lee, seeing a letter in *Mist's Journal* for 2 August 1718 complaining of the brutal treatment received by Hendley at Orpington (on a previous occasion), decided that it must have been written by Defoe and was led thereby to ascribe the present pamphlet to him, as "one of his ablest minor productions". In fact, Hendley, a well-known divine (and presumably capable of writing his own account of his troubles) was arrested on 25 October 1719 for writing the present tract, and he, his printer and his publisher Bickerton spent a night in the cells on its account. Characteristically, Moore, though aware of this fact, did not see it as a reason for rejecting Lee's attribution and surmised that the tract must be a case of collaboration: Defoe must have been called in to "prepare for the press an account of local Whig tyranny which had been sketched out by a High-Churchman". See our article, "Defoe, William Hendley and *Charity Still a Christian Virtue* (1719)", *HLQ*, 56 (1993), 327–30.

422 The Dumb Philosopher

London: Printed for Tho. Bickerton, 1719

ATTRIBUTION: Chalmers; Wilson, Lee, Trent (*CHEL*), Hutchins, Novak (as "Always attributed to Defoe but not certainly his").

An account of Dickory Cronke, a tinner's son of Cornwall who was born dumb but acquired speech just before he died, giving some of his private "Meditations" and his prophecies.

Rodney Baine, in *Daniel Defoe and the Supernatural* (Athens, Georgia, 1968), pp. 181–97, presents convincing arguments against this attribution.

423 The Petition of Dorothy Distaff

This entry was superseded by item **424a**.

424 The King of Pirates: Being an Account of the Famous Enterprises of Captain Avery

London: Printed for A. Bettesworth, C. King, J. Brotherton, W. Meadows, W. Chetwood, and Sold by W. Boreham, 1720 [for 1719]

ATTRIBUTION: Lee; Trent (*CHEL*), Hutchins, Moore, Novak.

Two narrative "Letters" from Captain Avery the pirate, telling the story of his settlement at Madagascar, his capture of the Mogul princess (though denying any ill-treatment of her) and his eventual return to Constantinople, disguised as an Armenian merchant. (The implication is that he is still alive.) It repudiates all earlier accounts as mere "romance".

Lee's attribution seems to have been based, partly, on the assumption that Defoe was hastily exploiting the success of *Robinson Crusoe*. The tract is, in fact, a rambling and ill-written affair, with many pages of tedious navigation details, though it comes to life in the description of the capture of the Mogul princess. It is largely devoid of ideas, differing in this from Defoe's known narratives, so that one would really want more definite evidence for his authorship. Moore appears not to have questioned Lee's ascription, though he is at pains to explain why there is a different and incompatible account of Avery in the *General History of the Pyrates*, which he also ascribes to Defoe (**458**, *q.v.*).

Several questions would need to be answered by anyone making a case for Defoe's authorship. For instance, why the account of Avery's exploits in *Captain Singleton*, published only a few months later, conflicts in some details with the one given here; and why more is not made of the suggestion that Avery might have paid the British Government a ransom for his pardon, a topic to which a whole issue of the *Review* was devoted in October 1707.

For a further discussion, see our *Canonisation*, pp. 102, 107–8.

424a The Female Manufacturers Complaint: Being the Humble Petition of Dorothy Distaff ... to the Lady Rebecca Woollpack

London: Printed for W. Boreham, 1720

ATTRIBUTION: Moore; Novak.

A response to Steele's anonymous *The Spinster: In Defence of the Woollen Manufactures*, 1 (1719), in which the "spinster" Rebecca Woolpack says that she is on the Wool, as opposed to the Calico, side in the current "Calico" controversy, but that she invites letters from any gentlewoman on the Calico side. Steels describes the costume of a modern English lady, practically every item in which comes, unpatriotically, from abroad.

The present "petition" by the Suffolk spinster Dorothy Distaff and her friends tells Mrs.Woolpack how the vogue for Indian calico is ruining their occupation and their chances of marriage. Dorothy implores Mrs. Woolpack to give up this new fashion rather than find herself ordered to do so by her husband or by Parliament, so letting down the cause of women. It concludes with a brief "Epistle" to Steele, dated 2 January 1720, from "Tisserando de Brocade", reminding him of various items of a lady's costume he omitted to mention and telling him that ladies who demand that all their clothes be French will find that French-style equivalents are now manufactured in Spitalfields.

Defoe was unquestionably closely involved in the Calico controversy and it is not impossible that he could have written this piece, but we have detected no really significant verbal echoes of his known writings on the subject. The parallel between "your Fancy... does now run for the Gewgaws of the *East Indies*" (p. 15) and the reference to "a whole Nation dress'd up in a new Gewgaw of Painted Callicoes" in the *Manufacturer* for 9 December 1719 is too vague to base anything on. Thus the only definite grounds for connecting Defoe with this piece is the fact that *Mercurius Politicus*, with which he is known to have been connected, reprinted it approvingly in its issue for December 1719, pp. 294–303. This does not seems sufficient grounds for an attribution.

425 An Historical Account of the Voyages and Adventures of Sir Walter Raleigh

London: Printed and Sold by W. Boreham, 1719 [1720]

ATTRIBUTION: Crossley; Trent (*Nation*), Hutchins, Moore, Novak.

The tract is in two parts. The first is a defence of Raleigh's career by one who has "the Honour to be related to his Blood" and can report family traditions about him. Its main drift is to assert what a noble inspiration on Raleigh's part it was to contemplate annexing Guiana, "the Richest, most Populous, and most Fertile Country in the World; a Country richer in Gold and Silver than *Mexico* and *Peru*; full of Inhabitants like *Great-Britain* it self; among whom an infinite Consumption of our Woollen Manufactures might have been expected" (p. 41). The second part proposes that the South Sea Company should undertake the conquest of Guiana but announces that, if it is unwilling, "another Set of Men... will be found ready to form a Subscription of a Million Sterling for such an Undertaking" (pp. 44–45). The author is "ready to lay before them a Plan or Chart of the Rivers and Shores, the Depths of Water, and all necessary Instructions for the Navigation, with a Scheme of the Undertaking, which he had the Honour about thirty Years ago, to lay before King *William*" (p. 55). Both parts quote extensively from Raleigh's famous *Discovery of the Large, Rich, and Beautiful Empire of Guiana* (1596).

Noting that, in *A General History of Discoveries and Improvements* (1725), Defoe specifically remarked (pp. 276–67) that any project of permanent conquest of Guiana was doomed to failure, and moreover that on several occasions he put forward detailed proposals for a colony in southern Chile, we argued in the *Canonisation* (pp. 164–67) that the present tract was most probably just a fraudulent "South Sea Bubble" prospectus. However, since then we have come across a passage in the *Manufacturer*, a periodical of which there is strong reason to believe Defoe the author, which casts a rather different light on the matter. It appears in the issue for 10 August 1720 and runs:

> I am for prompting Merchants to rational and probable Adventures, and Sailors to new Discoveries: These are all Things valuable in their Nature, solid in their Design and gloriously advantageous in their Success.
>
> By seeking out such Adventures and Discoveries, all our Increase in Colonies and Plantations has been produc'd: 'Twas by such happy Attempts, that the famous Sir *Walter Raleigh* and his Assistants settled the *British* Nation upon the Northern Continent of *America*; and, had he been encourag'd, or rather, had he not been basely betray'd, he had settled us also upon the Southern Continent too; and ... the *South-Sea* had been our own, and all the Wealth and Glory of *America*, paid Homage to King *George*.
>
> But Fate, and the ill Politicks of those Times hinder'd, and the Golden Mountains of *Chili*, the Silver Mines of *Potosi*, the Wealth of the richest Part of the World, is sacrific'd to the Lust and Sloth of the poorest and proudest Nation under the Sun ... These noble Designs, these glorious Undertakings cannot be call'd Projects, cannot be call'd Bubbles, *no, no*, far from it; nor, as I can find, did all our Bubble-Projectors ever propose one Subscription for making Discoveries ...
>
> Why has no bold Undertaker follow'd the glorious Sir *Walter Raleigh* up the River of *Amazon*, the *Rio Parano*, and the Great *Oroonoque*, where thousands of Nations remain undiscover'd, and where the Wealth, the Fruitfulness of the Soil, the goodness of the Climate, and the infinite Numbers of the People, exceeds all that has ever been conquer'd or discover'd in the *American* World?

On the strength of this similarity, and the reference to laying a scheme before King William (see letter from Defoe to Harley, 23 July 1711, and *Review* for 19 July 1711), one is strongly tempted to assign the tract to the "probably by Defoe" category; but the reference to the author's being personally related to Raleigh, and the remark in the *General History of Discoveries* about the impossibility of conquering Guiana, are anomalies which still make the ascription somewhat too problematic.

427 The Case of the Fair Traders

[London, 1720?]

ATTRIBUTION: Moore; Novak ("Attributed to Defoe by J.R. Moore").

A petition to Parliament for action against illegal exports (of wool, etc.) and illicit relanding of imports (of pepper and calicoes) after "drawbacks" have been obtained, thereby defrauding the Treasury and injuring "fair traders".

Moore seems to have attributed this purely on the grounds that a paragraph from it is quoted in *The Trade to India Critically and Calmly Consider'd* (1720), a tract which there is reason to think is probably by Defoe. This scarcely seems sufficient basis for an attribution.

429 The Case Fairly Stated between the Turky Company and the Italian Merchants. By a Merchant

London: Printed for J. Roberts, 1720

ATTRIBUTION: Trent (*Nation*); Hutchins, Moore, Novak (as "Attributed to Defoe by J.R. Moore").

A detailed argument, written in the person of a Merchant, against the legislation currently being lobbied for by the Turkey Company to prevent the Italian merchants importing raw silk from France, via Leghorn. It attempts to show that the Turkey Company really wants to ruin the Italian merchants' trade with Turkey altogether and claims that, by its monopolistic ways, the Company is doing great damage to British commerce. The right solution, it says, would be free trade.

Trent can only bring his usual stylistic arguments to support this ascription of his (and by the time of his Bibliography he has convinced himself that Defoe also wrote a counterblast on behalf of the Turkey Company, entitled *The Turkey Merchants and their Trade Vindicated*). In the absence of other evidence connecting Defoe with the Italian merchants, the case for this attribution seems flimsy.

431 A Letter to the Author of the *Independent Whig*

London: Printed and Sold by A. Moore, 1720

ATTRIBUTION: Trent (*CHEL*; but not in his Bibliography); Moore, Novak (as "Perhaps by Defoe").

A facetious and jeering attack on the High-Church clergy, written in response to the "Author of the *Independent Whig*" by a layman "of a bulky Reputation", apparently (p. 29) belonging to the diocese of the Bishop of Oxford. It gives a rancorous account of the last years of Anne's reign, when "we had almost gone so far as to set a *Popish* Pretender on the Throne" – "But, ah! me, the Good Woman dy'd" (p. 17) – and proceeds to rehash the Bangorian controversy in knockabout fashion (pp. 22–32). On p. 22 we read: "we may judge of the Truth of what *Daniel d' Foe* says in one of his *Reviews*.

> Let it become a new proverbial Jest,
> To be as wicked as an *English* Priest."

Perhaps it was the reference to Defoe which encouraged Trent to attribute this to him, but if so it does not seem a good reason, and the flailing polemical tone never for a moment suggests Defoe.

432 The History of the Life and Adventures of Mr. Duncan Campbell

London: Printed for E. Curll and Sold by W. Mears, T. Jauncy, W. Meadows, A. Bettesworth, W. Lewis and W. Graves, 1720

ATTRIBUTION: Chalmers; Wilson, Lee, Trent (*CHEL*, as "Probably revised by William Bond"), Moore, Novak (as "Always attributed to Defoe, perhaps in part or entirely by Bond").

An account, written by a friend, of the life of the famous deaf-and-dumb seer Duncan Campbell, the son of a Highlander and a Lapland lady endowed with second sight. It describes his many remarkable feats of prediction after he took up residence in London, and includes discussion of such topics as sign language, second sight, natural magic and the existence of spirits.

Rodney Baine, in his *Daniel Defoe and the Supernatural* (Athens, Georgia, 1968), pp. 137–80, presents convincing arguments against this attribution and argues for William Bond as a more likely author.

433 The History of the Wars, of His Late Majesty Charles XII, King of Sweden

London: Printed by H.P. for A. Bell, W. Taylor and J. Osborn, 1720

ATTRIBUTION: Lee; Trent (*Nation*), Hutchins, Moore, Novak.

A second edition, including a lengthy "Continuation", of **322** (*q.v.*).

437 The South-Sea Scheme Examin'd

London: Printed for J. Roberts, 1720

ATTRIBUTION: Moore; Novak (as "Probably by Defoe").

A pamphlet, published at the beginning of October, attempting, by detailed financial calculations, to restore confidence in the South Sea stock, and pleading against a wilful running-down of credit.

As Boyer says in the *Political State* for October 1720 (pp. 361 and 365), this "Palliative Pamphlet" gives a strong impression of being inspired by the South Sea Company directors. It is very different in tone from the *Director*, which began publication on 5 October and which internal evidence indicates is probably by Defoe. Moreover, on 25 November the *Director* appears to be quoting its remark (p. 9) that if all the landowners of England were to attempt to sell their land they would find no buyer for it, despite its indisputable value – commenting that it is "no ill Simily", but there is "little else of Weight" in the pamphlet.

The case for assigning this to Defoe is flimsy.

438 A True State of the Contracts

London: Printed for J. Roberts, 1721

ATTRIBUTION: Moore; Novak.

A pamphlet, presumably published in March, taking the side of the "Sellers" in the dispute as to how the Third Money Subscription of the South Sea Company (opened in June or July 1720) should be wound up. At a meeting of the General Court of the South Sea Company in March 1721 it was debated whether contracts under the Third Subscription should be automatically rescinded (the subscribers being excused further payments and given South Sea stock at a given premium in respect of what they had already paid), or whether subscribers' acceptance of this arrangement should be optional. By a ballot, the former was agreed. This cancelling of contracts carried the implication that subscribers who had sold their subscriptions for ready money had had no right to do so and would be obliged to pay back what they had received from the "Buyers". The "Sellers" objected to this as an arbitrary infringement of their rights and demanded to be given "receipts" in respect of their contracts, calculated at a much higher premium (i.e. 1000 per cent). (There were several pamphlets published at this time on either side. See the *Political State* for March 1721, p. 241 *et seq.*)

The present pamphlet is a cogent statement of the "Sellers'" case by someone evidently closely involved, but we cannot guess why Moore should have ascribed it to Defoe.

439 A Vindication of the Honour and Justice of Parliament

London: Printed for A. More [1721]

ATTRIBUTION: Lee; Trent (*CHEL*), Hutchins, Moore, Novak.

An answer to *The Speech of the Right Honourable John Aislabie Esq.* (1721), pretending that this "Speech", dated 19 July 1721, cannot really be by Aislabie (the late Chancellor of the Exchequer, convicted by Parliament of fraudulent practices over the South Sea affair), since the case it makes is so weak and must be a libel. As Aislabie knows well himself, there was nothing unusual or improper in the Bill of Attainder brought against him, for Parliament does not have to observe the same procedural rules as a court of law. The author hopes in a few days to publish an account of the Gentleman who "Countenances, Caresses and encourages" the South Sea culprits.

We are aware of no solid evidence to connect this laborious and repetitive piece with Defoe. Lee, who mistakenly dates the tract back to February, takes literally the assertion that the "Speech" must be a libel and appears to believe that it helped prompt Defoe to write an essay on libels in *Applebee's Journal* on 15 July – a possibility ruled out by chronology. In vol. 2 of his *Life* Lee prints (as Defoe's) a facetious article from *Applebee's Journal* for 26 August 1721, announcing that a Problematick Society has been founded and that it had intended to debate "whether it has been better or worse for Mr. Aislabie, that he has suffer'd a *Pamphlet call'd a Speech, etc., to be publish'd*", but the Judges have already given a prize to the person who argued "*that a lame Defence of a bad Cause, makes that bad worse*". Lee's conviction that Defoe was a regular contributor to *Applebee's Journal* is, however, extremely suspect and it is not safe to place any reliance on it.

442 Some Account of the Life of Sir Charles Sedley

Prefixed to the *Works* of Sedley, 2 vols.; London: Printed for S. Briscoe and Sold by T. Bickerton, 1722

ATTRIBUTION: Hutchins; Moore, Novak.

A brief nine-page account of the life and character of the poet Sedley, telling of the pleasure that Charles II took in his company and his modesty in not pressing for rewards from the King. It praises his verse for its freedom from the grossness of Rochester and other contemporaries.

It is a puzzle why Hutchins attributed this to Defoe. (Presumably Moore simply took the attribution on trust.) It seems an implausible ascription, if only because it praises Sedley, whom one scarcely remembers Defoe referring to elsewhere, above Rochester, whom he never tired of quoting.

444 A Collection of Miscellany Letters, Selected out of *Mist's Weekly Journal*: The First Volume

London: Printed by N. Mist, 1722

ATTRIBUTION: Lee; Trent (*CHEL*), Hutchins, Moore, Novak.

A selection of 105 letters and articles reprinted from *Mist's Weekly Journal*, with a Dedication (to Mist's readers) and a Preface. In this latter Mist, who has spent the whole of 1721 in prison, explains how he conceived the idea of this collection, and its successor the Second Volume (**445**), to recoup his finances, and how a "judicious, learned and merry Friend" paid him him a visit in prison and insisted that Mist, who had originally intended to leave the work of editing to his "devils", must supply a Dedication and a Preface, these being the most important parts of a book. The rest of the Preface gives some account of the origin and authorship of the chosen articles. (The two volumes were published simultaneously on 6 January 1722.)

It is not impossible that Defoe wrote certain of the articles reprinted in the collection, but there seems no evidence to support Lee's claims that the friend who visited Mist in prison was Defoe and that Defoe both helped with the selection and wrote the Dedication and the "greater part" of the Preface. However, later bibliographers have gone along with him, though Trent, in his Bibliography, is satirical about Lee's confidence in deciding which pieces, precisely, were the work of Defoe. ("It is a pity Lee was not a college professor or a newspaper and magazine critic, two positions in which an ability to express positive opinions, whether according to knowledge or not, makes eminently for success, of a kind.") He also points out that Lee's list of Defoe's supposed contributions, on page 349 of vol. 1 of his *Life*, does not tally exactly with the articles he actually reprinted in vol. 2.

It is to be noted that, whereas Lee did not think Defoe had anything to do with the Third and Fourth Volumes, published in 1727, Moore included them also in his *Checklist*. See **491** and **492**.

445 A Collection of Miscellany Letters, Selected out of *Mist's Weekly Journal*: The Second Volume

London: Printed by N. Mist, 1722

ATTRIBUTION: Lee; Trent (*CHEL*), Hutchins, Moore, Novak.

See **444**.

450 A Brief Debate upon the Dissolving the Late Parliament

London: Printed for J. Roberts, 1722

ATTRIBUTION: Crossley; Trent (Bibliography), Hutchins, Moore, Novak.

A neat and ferocious satire, published during the general election of April 1722, ironically arguing that, despite certain popular recriminations against the late ministry, and suggestions that there might have been more effort made to convict the real authors of the South Sea scandal, the country will certainly want to re-elect the same statesmen, enabling them to "act the same Thing over again" (p. 20). For the beauty of this scheme is that it will relieve them from any need for further bribery. The King, who was graciously pleased to pass a law extending the life of the last Parliament, will no doubt be glad for these men to be re-elected, so that they can serve him with the same fidelity, and so will various courtiers, both male and female (p. 33).

It would not be impossible to imagine Defoe writing this seditious polemic, savage not only to Walpole but to the King, but one would need much more evidence than exists for making the attribution. Trent's reason for supporting this attribution, as explained in his Bibliography, is revealingly illogical: "During my search for the tract I assumed that Defoe was the author, not only because Crossley ascribed it to him, but because no other pamphlet on the subject of the dissolution seemed to be clearly Defoe's."

451 An Impartial History of the Life and Actions of Peter Alexowitz, the Present Czar of Muscovy ... Written by a British Officer in the Service of the Czar

London: Printed for W. Chetwood, J. Stagg, J. Brotherton and T. Edlin, 1723 [for 1722]

ATTRIBUTION: Crossley; Lee, Trent (*Nation*), Hutchins, Moore, Novak.

A lengthy and eulogistic account of the life and career of Peter the Great up to the time of his triumphal entry into St. Petersburg in September 1714. The author (p. 5) explains that no reliable information could be obtained from Russia, so that he has had to rely on reports published in other countries. There are some lengthy extracts from *History of the Wars ... of Charles XII* (1715), indicated by inverted commas, and mention is made of a variety of other sources, published and unpublished: e.g. "the Relations ... of some *Scots* Officers" (p. 10); "one Account ... which came by the way of *France*" (p. 24); "one of the Writers of that time" (p. 39). That the story is only taken up to 1714 no doubt reflects the fact that, otherwise, it would have been necessary to describe the enmity and conflict between George I and Peter the Great during the years 1716–18. (George regarded the Czar as his greatest enemy.)

This is, on several grounds, an implausible attribution. Defoe, in the *Review*, frequently criticised Peter the Great as a brutal despot (see the issues for 23 August 1711 and 18 March 1712), and a protest from the Czar once nearly got him into serious trouble. It thus seems unlikely that he would later have produced such a uniformly flattering biography. Moreover the work goes in for dutiful and laborious recitals of diplomatic receptions, royal ceremonial, processions and the like and devotes no less than forty pages to official exchanges over an insult to the Russian ambassador, whereas in his known writings Defoe tends to be slighting about diplomatic niceties and protocol. The conventionality of these pages, and the whole uncritical tenor of the book, are not suggestive of Defoe.

As regards the extracts from the *History of the Wars ... of Charles XII* (**322**, **433**, *qq.v.*), we consider it unlikely that Defoe wrote that work, but even were he to have done so, the employment of quotations from it hardly serves to prove him the author of the present one.

One fact alone seems to argue for Defoe's authorship. On p. 8 there is quoted a couplet from his *Reformation of Manners* (1702), "If Fools could their own Ignorance discern, / They'd be no longer Fools, because they'd Learn", which was a favourite of his and also appears in his *Serious Reflections of Robinson Crusoe*, his *System of Magick* and his *Complete English Gentleman*. This is a suggestive piece of evidence. However, it admits of other explanations (for instance that the author picked it up, as a handy tag, from *Serious Reflections*), and it hardly seems sufficient grounds, in itself, for ascribing this vast 420-page compilation to Defoe.

453 A Memorial to the Clergy of the Church of England

London: Printed for J. Roberts, 1723

ATTRIBUTION: Moore; Novak (as "Probably by Defoe").

An earnest lamentation and exhortation, addressed by a clergyman of the Church of England to his fellow-clergy, at the prospect of the forthcoming Atterbury trial. He tells them of the bad reputation they have acquired in recent years, as enemies of liberty and toleration, as turbulent, seditious and greedy for power, and as indifferent to religion and the validity of oaths.

It is straining the "Defoe in disguise" theory too hard to assign this platitudinous and sermonising piece to him.

*454 The Wickedness of a Disregard to Oaths

[London]: Printed in the Year 1723

ATTRIBUTION: Moore (as "Very probably, not certainly, by Defoe").

A laborious defence of the binding nature of the Oaths of Allegiance and Abjuration against the arguments of those who would deny the validity of oaths taken at the Revolution; and an exposition of the importance of oaths in general, as the basis of civil society. The tract is partly a reply to a Non-Juring document seized at the arrest of Lord North and Grey and printed in the report of the Select Committee investigating the Atterbury Plot.

One can see no good reason why Moore should have made this tentative attribution to Defoe. The sedate style never suggests him, and the fact that he would no doubt have given general approval to its sentiments is hardly in itself an argument for his authorship.

*455 Considerations on Publick Credit

London: Printed for J. Roberts, 1724

ATTRIBUTION: Trent (*CHEL*); Hutchins, Moore (as "Probably, not certainly, by Defoe").

A sober set of reflections on the nature of public credit and the importance of resuming the process, interrupted by the South Sea Bubble, of reducing the public debt by means of a reduction in the interest rate, the surplus going to a sinking fund. Argues that the distinction popularised a few years ago (by the Tories) between the "moneyed interest" and the "landed interest" is fallacious, the two interests being inextricably intertwined.

These are undoubtedly views held by Defoe, and Trent, at least, bases his ascription purely on compatibility with his outlook. But the style of the pamphlet – a series of short, single-sentence paragraphs – is not suggestive of Defoe, and probably no attribution ought to be made until more is known about his political activities, if any, at this period.

458 A General History of the ... Pyrates ... By Captain Charles Johnson

London: Printed for Ch. Rivington, J. Lacy and J. Stone, 1724

ATTRIBUTION: Moore, in *Defoe in the Pillory and Other Studies* (1939); Hutchins, Novak.

A very extensive collection of biographies of famous pirates (a leading source for all subsequent pirate literature).

Moore announced his belief that Defoe had a considerable hand in this work, described on its title-page as "by Captain Charles Johnson", at an MLA meeting in 1932; and by 1939, when he published *Defoe in the Pillory and Other Studies*, he was asserting that the *General History* was substantially Defoe's work throughout and that it combined much authentic information with passages of historical fiction and "unrestrained romance". His case was based entirely on internal evidence, and in particular on "parallels" with Defoe's known works. We have discussed this important attribution at some length in the *Canonisation*, pp. 100–9, and, as we say there, regard it as a signal example of Moore's faulty methods in Defoe attribution: his unconvincing way of dealing with unwelcome evidence, his tendency to "chain-forging", and the sheer weakness of his argument from "parallels".

462 The Royal Progress

London: Printed by John Darby and Sold by J. Roberts, J. Brotherton and A. Dodd, 1724

ATTRIBUTION: Crossley; Trent (*CHEL*), Hutchins, Moore, Novak.

A flowery disquisition, drawn from Eachard's *Roman History* (p. 4) and similar works, on the wisdom of certain rulers in the past – the Emperor Hadrian, François I, Henri IV, Queen Elizabeth, King William, etc. – in showing themselves to their people, by means of "progresses". The implicit message of the tract is that George I could well benefit from their example instead of escaping to Hanover at every opportunity.

It does not seem very profitable to search for reasons which might justify Crossley's ascription to Defoe of this long, bland and esentially banal tract. Until a case has been made for the ascription, it will be best to discount it.

463 [Letter about the King's Intended Progress]

Known only from Boyer's *Political State*, June 1724, 615–18

ATTRIBUTION: Moore; Novak.

A letter from an unnamed correspondent in Nottingham, dated 8 June 1724, asking Boyer whether there is any truth in the report that George I is planning to make a "progress" through the Midlands. The idea of such a desirable event has been put into his head by "a Book lately sent down here from *London*, call'd *The Royal Progress*"; and he relates a dream he had of the joyful reception of King George in Nottingham, "attended with the Flower of all the Nobility and Gentry of our side of *England*", and the discomfiture it caused to the local Jacobites.

Moore is clearly attributing this on the assumption that Defoe wrote *The*

Royal Progress (**462**, *q.v.*), which obliquely urges King George to make such a progress, but this is itself a dubious attribution.

464 [Two Letters to the Author of the *Flying-Post*]

Known only from Boyer's *Political State*, August 1724, 203–12

ATTRIBUTION: Moore (as "almost certainly by Defoe").

An attack in the form of two letters to the "Author" of the *Flying-Post* (reprinted in the *Political State* for August 1724) on the reprinting of the *Works* of Matthew Prior and the subscription list for this immoral production, which included an Archbishop, several Bishops and "a whole Cloud of Deans" etc.

The second paragraph begins: " 'Tis very well known that the immortal Daniel de Foe, for want of other Employment, did frequently write against himself, to keep the Wheels a going." This appears sufficient reason for dismissing the attribution as most implausible.

465 A Narrative of the Proceedings in France for Discovering and Detecting the Murderers of the English Gentlemen ... near Calais ... Translated from the French

London: Printed for J. Roberts, 1724

ATTRIBUTION: Lee; Trent (*CHEL*), Hutchins, Moore, Novak.

An account, described on the title-page as "Translated from the French", of the activities of Joseph Bizeau, a sometime associate of the famous brigand Cartouche, and of the murder of the Englishmen Sebright, Davies and Mompesson by Bizeau and his gang in September 1723. There are frequent references to a manuscript source, written by "a Person of Credit" (p. 11). On p. 88 there begins the report by Sebright's servant Richard Spindelow, who survived the attack and was taken back to Paris later to identify the murderers.

A report of the murders, as from the lips of Sebright's servant Spindelow, appeared in the *Political State* for September 1723. However when Lee, who was apparently unaware of this report, read an account of the murders in *Applebee's Journal* for 2 November 1723, he took it for granted that this was Defoe writing "as if from the mouth" of Spindelow. Accordingly he pictured Defoe – who, according to Lee's belief, had already been responsible for a *Life and Actions of Lewis Dominique Cartouche* (1722) – as having made further researches into French brigandage and publishing the present tract in August 1724, describing it as a translation to make it appear "better authenticated".

According to John Nichols's *Literary Anecdotes* (1812), i, 161–62, the *Narrative* was written by Dr. Samuel Jebb, who also composed the Latin inscription on the pyramid erected to commemorate the crime. There appears to be no particular reason to doubt the attribution to Samuel Jebb, and we have here a good example of the fatal consequences of Lee's conviction that he had identified Defoe as Applebee's leader-writer.

Moore presumably did not know of the Nichols attribution, though he must have been aware that George Aitken had found a French original of the *Life and Actions of Lewis Dominique Cartouche*, since he omitted it from his *Checklist*. See G.A. Aitken (ed.), *Romances and Narratives of Daniel Defoe*, 16 vols. (1895), xvi, pp. xi-xii.

466 A Narrative of all the Robberies, Escapes etc. of John Sheppard

London: Printed and Sold by John Applebee, 1724

ATTRIBUTION: Lee; Trent (*CHEL*), Hutchins, Moore, Novak.

A curious, naive and colourful account of Sheppard's brief life of crime and famous escapes, concluding with thanks to the various clergymen who visited him in prison. It explicitly refers to, and corrects as to matters of fact, the *History of the Remarkable Life of John Sheppard* (**468**, *q.v.*).

It would appear that Lee attributed this to Defoe purely on the basis of his theory that Applebee had acquired special privileges at Newgate and employed Defoe as his representative there, to interview prisoners and turn their confessions into newspaper articles and pamphlets. This whole elaborate construction of Lee's, based originally on certain articles in *Applebee's Journal* which he believed to be by Defoe, is deeply suspect and, so far as Defoe is concerned, unsupported by external evidence. It is not even plain that Applebee had privileged access to prisoners, though it true that he became the recognised publisher of the "Genuine Accounts of Last Confessions", as recorded by the Ordinary. Also it weakens Lee's account that he wants Defoe to be one of the "Gentlemen" who, according to a report in *Applebee's Journal*, 12 September, visited Sheppard in prison: that is to say, he wants it both ways, Defoe as hired reporter and Defoe as philanthropic saver of souls. See further our account in *Canonisation*, pp. 72–4.

There seems no good reason to connect the present pamphlet with Defoe – Lee's elaborate account of Defoe's relations with Sheppard being, so far as one can see, sheer fantasy.

467 Some Farther Account of the Original Disputes in Ireland, about Farthings and Halfpence: In a Discourse with a Quaker of Dublin

[London]: Printed in the Year 1724

ATTRIBUTION: Crossley; Trent (*Nation*), Hutchins, Moore, Novak.

A dialogue between an Irish Quaker, recently come to England, and the author, an Englishman, in which the Quaker convinces the author that the outcry against "Wood's Halfpence" in the Irish Parliament and the English press has been based on a total misunderstanding. The truth is, the Irish only objected because they wanted the patent for themselves. The new copper coinage was sorely needed; the patent was issued with very strict conditions; and Wood in fact intends to invest his profits in Irish linen, thus benefiting Ireland.

Crossley writes that this "most interesting tract" is written in opposition to Swift's *Drapier's Letters* and that the "evidence of Defoe's pen" is clear. However, all the indications seem to be that it refers (p. 23) to the controversy in the press in October 1723, i.e. four months before Swift entered the debate. There seems no good reason for assigning it to Defoe; and Michael Ryder, in his article "Defoe, Goode and Wood's Halfpence", *N & Q*, n.s., 30 (1983), 22–23, presents strong evidence for its being by Barnham Goode.

468 The History of the Remarkable Life of John Sheppard

London: Printed and Sold by John Applebee, J. Isted, and the Booksellers of London and Westminster [1724]

ATTRIBUTION: Lee; Trent (*CHEL*), Hutchins, Moore, Novak.

A lively, in places sensational, third-person account of Sheppard's career up to and including his escape from the "Castle" in Newgate on 15 October 1724, giving quite a lifelike sketch of his character and quoting some of his witticisms. There follows (pp. 51 *et seq.*) a fictitious letter from Sheppard, in burlesque style, and a hasty and perfunctory final paragraph.

It seems plain that Lee had never in fact seen a copy of this tract, for he gives no pagination and says, quite wrongly, that it gives only a "bare mention" of the final escape (Lee, i, 385), whereas it devotes several pages to it (pp. 40 *et seq.*). Thus he has ascribed it purely on the basis of his theory that Defoe wrote all Applebee's "crime" pamphlets. Moore also seems to have got into a muddle over the Sheppard tracts, for he gives what is evidently the earlier tract (i.e. the present one) a later number than its companion.

Sheppard's noisily facetious punning letter is in a style we have no reason to believe that Defoe ever practised; and altogether the case for ascribing this to him does not seem adequate.

*470 An Epistle from Jack Sheppard to the Late L[or]d C[hance]ll[o]r of E[nglan]d

[London]: Printed in the Year 1725

ATTRIBUTION: Moore (as "Perhaps, not certainly, Defoe's"); Novak (as "Perhaps by Defoe").

A satirical ballad on Lord Macclesfield, recently convicted of corruption.

Moore's arguments for the ascription, on the grounds that nobody except Defoe had all the interests revealed in this poem, do not convince. (The "Who but Defoe?" theory is always unsafe.) Moreover, there is reason to suppose that, rather than nursing a "deep personal grievance" against Lord Macclesfield (the one-time Lord Chief Justice Thomas Parker), Defoe regarded him with gratitude. See James Sutherland, *Defoe* (1937), p. 215; *Letters*, p. 451 and note.

471 The Life of Jonathan Wild ... By H.D. Late Clerk to Justice R[aymond]

London: Printed for T. Warner, 1725

ATTRIBUTION: Crossley; Trent (*Nation*), Hutchins, Moore, Novak.

A collection of anecdotes, purportedly from Wild's own lips and compiled, according to the title-page, by "H.D., late Clerk to Justice R– [Lord Chief Justice Raymond, who sentenced Wild to execution]", illustrating Wild's cunning devices during the days of his prosperity and his Machiavellian skill in erecting a "commonwealth" of thieves. The tract claims only to be relating facts that have not already been published in other pamphlets.

Quite a lively piece, making much play with thieves' cant ("a very *good Lay*", "*spoke with* a Silver Tankard", "the World was grown so *peery*", etc.), but giving no feel of being by Defoe. It is worth noting that George Aitken, who devoted considerable study to these "crime" pamphlets, rejected this Crossley attribution. See G.A. Aitken (ed.), *Romances and Narratives of Daniel Defoe*, 16 vols. (1895), xvi, p. xvi.

473 The True and Genuine Account ... of the Late Jonathan Wild

London: Printed and Sold by John Applebee, J. Isted and the Booksellers of London and Westminster, 1725

ATTRIBUTION: Lee (who, however, appears never actually to have seen a copy); Crossley, Trent (*CHEL*), Hutchins, Moore, Novak.

Published 8 June 1725, a very competently written account of the life and death of the notorious thief-catcher Jonathan Wild, who was executed on 24 May 1725. The author, who claims (p. 25) to have had personal dealings with Wild over some stolen property, says he regards Wild's story as a serious and tragic affair and does not intend to turn it into a joke, as some hack writers have done. The tract places much emphasis on Wild's business-like methods and on his breeding up of children as thieves. On pp. 26–28 there is a neat and vivid piece of dramatic dialogue. The Introduction says that the work was advertised some time ago, to prevent people being taken in by inferior and spurious productions.

It seems plain that Lee assigned this to Defoe merely on the strength of his supposed connection with the publisher John Applebee, which must be regarded as a very speculative hypothesis (see next item).

The only detail which might be thought definitely to point to Defoe is the phrase "talking *Gospel* to a kettle Drum" (p. 31), which was certainly one of his favourites. However, it is linked here to two other proverbial catch-phrases, "bidding a Dragoon not Plunder" and "talking of Compassion to a Hussar", which implies that it is a common saying.

Altogether, though it would not be absurd to attribute this to Defoe, there hardly seems sufficient grounds for doing so.

474 An Account of the Conduct ... of the Late John Gow

London: Printed and Sold by John Applebee [1725]

ATTRIBUTION: Lee; Trent (*CHEL*), Hutchins, Moore, Novak.

Gives a fairly detailed account of John Gow's beginnings as a pirate, the murder of the officers of the *George* under his leadership, his rovings on the high seas and his return to the Orkneys, where he and his gang are outwitted and captured by his old schoolfriend James Fea. It is competently written, though the narrative of the final capture tends to get confused.

Lee attributed this work on the strength of his belief that Defoe had a connection with Applebee which gained him special access to condemned criminals (see *Life*, i, 399). Moore, for his part, spent much vain effort in trying to prove that the present tract and the account of Gow in the *General History of the Pyrates* (**458**, *q.v.*) were by the same author, despite their differences and contradictions. (See *Canonisation*, p. 103.) A significant fact that he does not mention, however, is that the present tract, unlike the *General History* account, makes no reference to Gow's sweetheart, who normally plays an important part in the Gow legend (as for instance in the sources drawn on by Walter Scott in his novel *The Pirate*).

All in all, neither Lee's nor Moore's dealings with this pamphlet carry conviction, and its authorship must remain an open question.

478 A Brief Historical Account of the Lives of the Six Notorious Street-Robbers

London: Printed for A. Moore, 1726

ATTRIBUTION: Crossley; Trent (*CHEL*), Hutchins, Moore, Novak.

An account, published on 6 April 1726, of the six street-robbers Blewet, Bunworth, Dickenson, Berry, Higges and Legee executed at Kingston on that day. It notes that the gang to which the six belonged represented a new kind of civic danger, being murderers as well as thieves, and reports the rumours that the gang was planning some alarming "*coup d'eclat*". The tract deals mainly with William Blewet, expounding his rules for the art of sword-stealing and relating how he took refuge in Holland, accompanied by Dickenson and Berry, where they were at last arrested at the instigation of the British Minister at the Hague. It also describes how Bunworth, after suffering torture by "pressing", was at last induced to plead.

There is nothing in the style and approach of this tract to distinguish it markedly from the *True and Exact Account of the Lives of Edward Burnworth alias Frasier, William Blewitt, Thomas Berry, and Emanuel Dickenson* published at much the same time by John Applebee. On p. 19, however, it mentions gangs of "poor Vagabond-boys, who having neither Father or Mother, House or Home to retreat to, creep at Night into the Ash-holes of the nealing Arches of the Glass-Houses, where they lie for the Benefit of the Warmth of the Place". This seems somewhat to echo *Colonel Jack* (Oxford English Novels Edition, 1965, p. 9): "in Winter we got into the Ash-holes, and Nealing Arches in the Glass-house". But since it is always possible that the author borrowed this detail from *Colonel Jack*, the resemblance can hardly be regarded as clinching evidence for Defoe's authorship.

481 Unparallel'd Cruelty

London: Printed for T. Warner, 1726

ATTRIBUTION: Crossley; Trent (*CHEL*), Hutchins, Moore, Novak.

An account of the hideous and repellent tortures inflicted by Captain Jeane of Bristol on his cabin-boy and of Jeane's imprisonment, execution (13 May 1726) and hanging-up in chains at Greenwich. On p. 18 it is stated that the High Constable, having read Jeane's speech to the crowd at his hanging, gave it to Applebee the printer, who published the substance of it in *Applebee's Weekly Journal* for 14 May – the present tract also being based on it.

It is not plain what could have prompted Crossley to assign this piece of sensational journalism to Defoe.

482 The Friendly Daemon ... Being a True Narrative of a Miraculous Cure, Newly Perform'd upon that Famous Deaf and Dumb Gentleman, Dr. Duncan Campbell

London: Printed and Sold by J. Roberts, 1726

ATTRIBUTION: Wilson (as "Most probably" by Defoe); Lee, Trent (*CHEL*), Hutchins, Moore, Novak.

The celebrated deaf-and-dumb seer Duncan Campbell writes to an unnamed friend and physician, describing how in the year 1717 he began to be incapacited by fits, becoming incapable of communicating with his clients, but how in 1724, as he lay in bed in the morning, a familiar spirit or "genius" appeared to him, clothed in a surplice like a choirboy, and gave him a prescription for his ailment – involving magnets and a sympathetic powder. His friend replies, citing various cases in which similar semi-miraculous remedies have proved successful. A postscript informs readers that the sympathetic powder may be obtained at Dr. Campbell's house in Buckingham Court, near Charing Cross.

Rodney Baine, in his *Daniel Defoe and the Supernatural* (Athens, Georgia, 1968), pp. 146–47, brings convincing arguments against this attribution.

483 The Four Years Voyages of Capt. George Roberts ... Written by Himself

London: Printed for A. Bettesworth and J. Osborn, 1726

ATTRIBUTION: Wilson (who reports it as an attribution suggested by a friend, on which he himself cannot express a firm opinion, iii, 543); Trent (*CHEL*), Hutchins, Moore, Novak.

A lengthy (458-page) first-person narrative by Roberts, describing his capture by the pirate Low, who sets him adrift in a sloop with only two boys for crew, and his subsequent shipwreck and adventures among the Cape Verde Islands. The last hundred pages or so are given over to a factual account of the mode of life and industry of the inhabitants of each of the islands. The book is dedicated to "William Killet, of Gorlestown in the County of Suffolk", and a note at the end states that one of the boys who accompanied Roberts "now lives with Mr. *Galapin*, a Tobacconist, in *Monument Yard*, and may be referred to for the Truth of most of the Particulars before related".

The only extended discussions of the attribution to Defoe are in Trent's unpublished Bibliography, and in J.R. Moore's *Defoe in the Pillory and Other Studies* (Bloomington, Indiana, 1939), pp. 169–77. Trent confesses that for a long time he doubted Defoe's authorship, partly because of a lack of "special features" of his style, but also because of the dullness of the book. Gradually, however, he became convinced, despite these difficulties. The wilful self-persuasion by which he reached this conclusion is evident in the following extract from his lengthy commentary:

> I am sure, after once scouting such notions, that Daniel Defoe wrote or compiled or edited or had some sort of connnection with *The Four Years Voyages of Capt. George Roberts*. He may have been supplied with materials by that worthy sailor – particularly with nautical details – or he may have made up the adventures and stolen the descriptions of the islands from as yet undetermined books in English or French. His manuscript may have passed through the hands of someone who carefully wrote "nor" and "whom" and cut out obtrusive phrases like "I say" and "in short". Or he may have incorporated the notes of which Roberts speaks, or large portions of that worthy's

manuscript in the copy that went finally to the printers. On these points I have no decided opinion. I am merely confident that it was in the main Defoe who described Roberts's attempt to climb the cliff, and his illness, and his building his boat, and his subsequent adventures among the islands. I base my belief largely on the way the conversations are reported and on the nature and the handling of the details. If the book were only fifty or a hundred pages long, I could not be sure that I was not reading the work of an imitator; but in four hundred and fifty pages the difference between a master and an imitator is almost sure to emerge to a close student, and I think it emerges here.

Moore, for his part, had no doubt that *The Four Years Voyages* "is clearly a work of fiction based (like all Defoe's fiction) on a considerable amount of fact". He, too, admits that "the story is less interesting than most of Defoe's works", but his concern is not so much to establish the attribution as to explain the intricate relationship between this work and *A General History of the Pyrates* (1724) (**458**, *q.v.*), the latter being in Moore's eyes a much more significant addition to the Defoe canon. As we argue in our *Canonisation* (pp. 104–5), Moore's discussion of the two works is a prime example of "chain-forging" – one tentative attribution being used to support another – and his attempts at explaining away significant discrepancies between the two works are singularly unconvincing.

485 Some Considerations upon Street-Walkers ... To Which is Added, a Letter from One of those Unhappy Persons

London: Printed for A. Moore [1726]

ATTRIBUTION: Trent (*CHEL*); Hutchins, Moore, Novak.

A sententious and "improving" appeal to a Member of Parliament to do something to lessen the intolerable nuisance and scandal of street-walkers. It would appear, says the author, that English harlots are unique in resorting to no disguise, or even pretence of modesty. There is, he says, probably a middle solution between indulgence and the licensing of brothels and extreme severity towards fornication in general. The ancient Hebrews and Romans used methods of control which it might be possible to learn from, and some Roman moralists praised young men for resorting to brothels rather than molesting married women. Why should not Parliament grant tax-relief and other privileges to married parents?

There is no particular verbal resemblance between this and the brief passage on street-walkers in the "Andrew Moreton" pamphlet *Augusta Triumphans* (1728), pp. 27–28, and it is hard to see any compelling reason for assigning it to Defoe. Trent merely falls back on his "tests".

(Moore seems to be in a slight confusion over the pamphlet, since, in the note in his *Checklist*, he mistakenly implies that it is listed by Lee.)

491 A Collection of Miscellany Letters, Selected out of *Mist's Weekly Journal*: The Third Volume

London: Printed for T. Warner, 1727

ATTRIBUTION: Moore.

See **444**.

492 A Collection of Miscellany Letters, Selected out of *Mist's Weekly Journal*: The Fourth Volume

London: Printed for T. Warner, 1727

ATTRIBUTION: Moore.

See **444**.

500 The Memoirs of an English Officer ... By Capt. George Carleton

London: Printed for E. Symon, 1728

ATTRIBUTION: Wilson (a tentative attribution); Trent (*CHEL*), Hutchins, Moore, Novak (as "Always attributed to Defoe, but possibly in part by a real G. Carleton").

An account by George Carleton of his military experiences in the Dutch War and the War of the Spanish Succession, in the latter of which he served in Spain. He eulogises his general, Lord Peterborough.

Wilson, writing soon after Walter Scott's edition of the *Memoirs* of 1808, which raised no doubts about Carleton's authorship, decided (iii, 589) that "it is probable that De Foe has the best title to authorship", on the grounds that the work was a fiction, resembling *Memoirs of a Cavalier* etc. Lee rejected it. Colonel A. Parnell, a historian, found out a great deal about George Carleton, who served in the wars as the book claims, but concluded that the work was written by Swift, on the basis of information from Carleton and Carleton's kinsman Villar Carleton; see "Dean Swift and the *Memoirs of Captain Carleton*", *English Historical Review*, 6 (1891), 97–151. Trent, who has a long and amusing discussion of the work, thought that Defoe had a large hand in it. Moore says that a copy owned by Sir Harold Williams has manuscript notes to the effect that Carleton "hung round the press" while the book was being printed and introduced some "ffoists" of his own, but he asserts that "This only strengthens the certainty that Defoe was the author, using the name of Carleton for his own purpose". This reasoning of Moore's, in so far as it concerns Defoe, is plainly illogical.

Rodney Baine brings strong arguments against Defoe's authorship in "Daniel Defoe and Captain Carleton's *Memoirs of an English Officer*", *Texas Studies in Literature and Language*, 13 (1972), 613–27, and, after exhaustive study, Steig Hargevik also rejects the attribution; see his *The Disputed Assignment of "Memoirs of an English Officer" to Daniel Defoe*, 2 vols. (Stockholm, 1972, 1974).

502 An Impartial Account of the Late Famous Siege of Gibralter ... By an Officer

London: Printed for T. Warner, 1728

ATTRIBUTION: Trent (*CHEL*); Hutchins, Moore, Novak.

An account by an "Officer", who claims to have been a participant, of the siege of Gibraltar during the brief war between Britain and Spain in 1727. It contains various documents, much military detail, lists of officers etc. and tells how two Moorish spies were executed and their flayed skin hung up as a warning – a portion of their skin being on show at the publisher's office (p. 37). On p. 41 the author passes a satirical comment on "*Concise Elegant Writers*, or rather *Forgers* of Voyages".

Trent writes in his Bibliography, "it is only a strong general conviction of our pamphleteer's proximity – the smell of the snake, shall I dare call it? – that keeps me from relegating the unimportant performance to the 'strongly suspected' items". Boyer, who gave an abstract in the *Political State* for July 1728, was convinced that it was "written by a Gentleman of the Sword" (p. 33).

The case for a Defoe attribution seems extremely flimsy.

504 Street-Robberies, Consider'd ... Written by a Converted Thief

London: Printed for J. Roberts [1728]

ATTRIBUTION: Crossley (in *N & Q,* 1st series, 3 (1851), 195); Lee, Trent (*CHEL*), Moore, Novak.

The main body of the text is a waggish picaresque account of the author's apprenticeship and career as a thief, plentifully sprinkled with thieves' cant and incorporating a dictionary of "The Canting Language". This is followed by a scheme for preventing street-robberies and three brief treatises on theft. The first of the three treatises has been identified as deriving from John Clavell's *Recantation of an Ill Led Life* (1628).

Nothing in the autobiographical part suggests the author of *Moll Flanders*; nor does it seem likely that Defoe would have published so different a scheme for preventing street-robberies only a few days after the publication of *Second Thoughts are Best*. We firmly endorse the opinion of Clinton S. Bond, in "*Street-Robberies, Consider'd* and the Canon of Daniel Defoe", *Texas Studies in Literature and Language*, 13 (1971), 431–45, that this is an implausible attribution.

505 Reasons for a War

London: Printed for A. Dodd, R. Walker, E. Nutt and E. Smith, 1729

ATTRIBUTION: Lee; Trent (*CHEL*), Hutchins, Moore, Novak.

A bellicose tract, saying that the state of suspense as regards Spain's intentions has gone on for too long. The People are restless, and there is nothing seditious in suggesting that the King ought to take account of this, as indeed he appears to be doing. A war is always a calamity, but Spain is not an enemy to be feared, and a conflict with her is likely to turn out to Britain's advantage. For one thing, it will put a curb on her interference with Britain in the West Indies. "The Pulse of the Nation beats high for a War" (p. 13), and it is probably the only way to clear the air.

The tone and approach of this tract conflict at every point with those of a pamphlet which appeared only a couple of months later, *The Advantages of Peace and Commerce* (Moore, **510**), which there is good reason to think is by Defoe. Perhaps the only reason for considering the possibility of Defoe's authorship is that there are some reminiscences of a tract published two years earlier, *The Evident Approach of a War* (Moore, **488**), which there is reason to think is probably by Defoe. Both tracts carry the tag "*Pax* *quaeritur bello"* on their title-page, and there are a couple of similar wordings (compare pp. 8 and 23 with **488**, pp. 53 and 48). However, one can easily imagine the author of the present work as having borrowed from the earlier one.

506 The Unreasonableness and Ill Consequences of Imprisoning the Body for Debt

London: Printed and Sold by T. Read and J. Purser, 1729

ATTRIBUTION: Trent (Bibliography); Hutchins, Moore, Novak.

An expansion of *Vox Dei et Naturae* (1711), **199a**, *q.v.*

508 An Enquiry into the Pretensions of Spain to Gibralter

London: Printed for R. Walker, 1729

ATTRIBUTION: Trent (*CHEL*); Hutchins, Moore, Novak.

Published in April or May 1729, a jingoistic tract, endorsing the resolution in the House of Lords on 18 March against Britain's giving up Gibraltar to Spain, as certain of her allies would favour. The case is argued on the grounds that the King's right to Gibraltar under the terms of the Treaty of Utrecht is unquestionable. As for the importance of Gibraltar, it is probably more important for the Spanish to have than for Britain to lose. The supposed letter from George I envisaging the giving up of Gibraltar – a favourite topic of the day in coffee-houses – may well not be genuine, and at all events it does not contemplate an immediate handing over without further discussion. The author is sceptical about current talk of an "equivalent" for Gibraltar being offered by Spain.

This tract bears a close resemblance to the bellicose *Reasons for a War* (**505**, *q.v.*), and the same arguments against Defoe's authorship would apply.

511 Madagascar: or, Robert Drury's Journal

London: Printed and Sold by W. Meadows, J. Marshall, W. Worrall, "and by the Author, at Old Toms's Coffee-House in Birchin Lane", 1729

ATTRIBUTION: Trent (*CHEL*: "There is a strong probability that Defoe had a large share in this book"); Hutchins, Moore, Novak (as "Edited and written in part by Defoe").

The journal of Robert Drury, son of a London inn-keeper (edited for the press by a "Transcriber" and certified as truthful by a certain Captain William Mackett). It tells how Drury embarked at the age of fourteen on an East Indiaman named the *Degrave*, which was wrecked off the coast of Madagascar, Drury being captured and enslaved by the natives, spending some fifteen years on the island before being rescued by Captain Mackett.

Moore wrote a chapter about *Madagascar* in *Defoe in the Pillory and Other Studies* (Bloomington, Indiana, 1939) and a complete monograph on it, *Defoe's Sources for Robert Drury's Journal* (Bloomington, Indiana, 1943), his theory being that there had never been a journal by Drury, the whole book being a work of fiction by Defoe. He was challenged by A.W. Secord, who, in his posthumous *"Robert Drury's Journal" and Other Studies* (Champaign, Illinois, 1961), provided abundant evidence for the historical truth of the events described. The attempt to associate Defoe with this fascinating work appears supererogatory.

We discussed this attribution at some length in our *Canonisation*, pp. 109–13. Since then, important fieldwork in Madagascar by archaeologists and anthropologists has confirmed the authenticity of much of Drury's account of his experiences. In particular, the lost site of the ancient capital of the Antandroy in southern Madagascar, referred to by Drury as "Fenno-arevo", has been discovered. See M. Parker Pearson, "Tombs and Monumentality in Southern Madagascar: Preliminary Results of the Central Androy Survey", *Antiquity*, 66 (1992), 941–48; M. Parker Pearson, K. Godden, Retsihisatse Ramilisonina and J-L. Schwenninger, "Finding Fenoarivo: Fieldwork in Central Androy", *Nyame Akuma*, 41 (in press).

515 The Perjur'd Free Mason Detected

London: Printed for T. Warner, 1730

ATTRIBUTION: Crossley; Trent (*CHEL*), Hutchins, Moore, Novak.

An attack, in the person of a Freemason, on Samuel Pritchard's recent *Masonry Detected*, which had been reprinted in *Read's Weekly Journal* for 24 October 1730. It begins with a potted history of Freemasonry, after which there are several imaginary dialogues, between a Neophyte and a Master

Mason and between Samuel Pritchard and a "True Mason", in which Pritchard finds spurious reasons to defend his breaking his oath of secrecy and (like the Neophyte) complains that he had expected money from the Masons and got none, so has good reason to be revenged on them.

Trent, in his *Nation* articles, said he was inclined to follow George Aitken in rejecting this, but he proceeded to list it in the *Cambridge History of English Literature* (1912). Moore quotes the Deputy Town Clerk of Stoke Newington as saying, in *Daniel Defoe in Stoke Newington* (1960), that Defoe was "associated with the masonic lodge which met at the 'Three Crowns', on the corner of Church Street and High Street, and wrote a pamphlet attacking Pritchard the renegade free-mason". However, the reference to the pamphlet is evidently merely an echo of the Crossley-Trent attribution.

Defoe attacked Freemasonry in *An Essay on the History and Reality of Apparitions* (1727), p. 43, and in *Second Thoughts are Best* (1729), and there seems no strong reason to associate him with the present tedious and foolish piece.

516 An Effectual Scheme for the Immediate Preventing of Street Robberies

London: Printed for J. Wilford, 1731 [for 1730]

ATTRIBUTION: Crossley, in *N & Q*, 1st series, 3 (1851), 195; Lee, Trent (*CHEL*), Hutchins, Moore, Novak.

An argument, addressed by its author "J.R." to the new Lord Mayor of London, that all the previous schemes put forward for suppressing street-robberies (for instance by strengthening the Watch) have proved totally ineffectual. The only way to deal with the problem is to attack it at its source, i.e. to suppress the infamous "Night-houses" where prostitutes and robbers lurk and young lads are bred up as pickpockets. A little is being done in Westminster, with the King's encouragement, but the author prays that the reform should become universal.

This tract (see pp. 27–28 and 47–49) directly criticises past schemes of reform, such as those put forward in Defoe's *Augusta Triumphans* and *Second Thoughts are Best*, a fact which must cast doubt on the attribution.

517 The Voyage of Don Manoel Gonzales ... Translated from the Portugueze Manuscript

Published in vol. I of *A Collection of Voyages and Travels* compiled from material in the Harleian Collection by Thomas Osborne, London, 1745

ATTRIBUTION: Moore.

A long and detailed description of England by a Portuguese traveller.

Moore, in *Defoe in the Pillory and Other Studies* (Bloomington, Indiana, 1939), pp. 74–103, shows that many passages in this are close or identical to Defoe's *Tour*. However, as he admits, much more of the book corresponds closely to Guy Miege's *The Present State of Great Britain and Ireland* (1707). It is hard to see any good reason why, if the "Miege" passages are to be explained as plagiarism, the "Defoe" ones should not.

Index of Titles